Learning to Weave

Learning to Weave
A Woman-Loving Life

Jennie Boyd Bull

Mountain River Press
Burnsville, North Carolina

The names of two women and references to the author's Indian meditation path have been changed to honor their privacy. Otherwise, all names and places are accurate to the best of the author's ability.

Photographers have given permission and are credited, when known.

Front cover photo is a woven napkin by Jennie Boyd Bull.
Back cover author photo by Alice Aldrich.

Book design and layout by Diana Donovan
Celo Book Production Service
Burnsville, NC 28714

Paperback ISBN: 978-0-578-94367-1
eBook ISBN: 978-0-578-94368-8

Library of Congress Control Number: 2021913640

Copyright © 2021 by Jennie Boyd Bull
All rights reserved.

No part of this book may be reproduced or transmitted in any form or by any means, electronic or mechanical, including photocopying, recording, or by any information storage and retrieval system, without the permission of the Author, except for the use of brief quotations in a book review. To request permission, contact the publisher at:
MountainRiverPress@gmail.com

Distributed by Ingram and Indiebound.
Also available from Malaprops Bookstore, Asheville, NC and from Mountain River Press
50 Passional Way
Burnsville, NC 28714
MountainRiverPress@gmail.com

The weaving of my life is an unfolding, stretching, exploring, shifting, burning, softening search for Truth and integrity as a woman, as a Spirit-filled soul. I flow through many patterns—lesbian activist, pastor, editor, devotee, volunteer—as I weave in and out of a rainbow of purple, blue, and golden threads. I weave a circular flow of tender loves and generous communities, evolving projects and challenging politics, rugged mountain trails and fresh purple pansies, always seeking greater understanding and higher Truth. I am the resilient weaver I was born to be in this life. Let this fabric be my shroud.

—Jennie Boyd Bull

Contents

Acknowledgments	ix
Prologue: Weaving a Life	1
1 Beaming the Warp	3
2 Warp Threads	14
3 Women's Warp	19
4 Rainbow Weft	29
5 New Weave	39
6 Torn Weave	45
7 Radiant Weft	55
8 Fiery Weft	63
9 Whole Fabric	68
10 Flowing Weave	76
11 Remnants	87
Epilogue: Tying Off	94
Works Cited	96
About the Author	99

Acknowledgments

I'm grateful for the Great Smokies Writing Program creative nonfiction courses taught by Catherine Reid in 2016, 2017, and 2018, which inspired me to write this memoir. Many of these chapters were first written as essays for those classes.

The ongoing support of the Breezeway poetry and critique group hosted by Anne Maren-Hogan here in the South Toe River Valley continues to encourage me. I especially thank Kathy Weisfeld and Mendy Knott, whose 2018 critiques of the manuscript provided valuable guidance. Patricia Bernarding copyedited the manuscript with her focused attention to detail. Diana Donovan provided essential and skilled editing, design, production, and publishing assistance.

In 2021, reconnecting with longtime friend Sharon Deevey inspired me to resume editing and publication of this memoir by reminding me that our lesbian lives and spiritual seeking as women must be told and archived. This book is my contribution to that history.

Prologue
Weaving a Life

I weave the later years of my life in the mountains of Western North Carolina, in a pointy-roof green house by a stream, with goats next door. Tomatoes and basil grow out back.

At the end of the counter in my 750-square foot mountain home stands a simple, four-shaft loom, patiently waiting for me to unravel its mysteries. Weaving is a traditional craft of the Southern mountains. Like many women here before me, I want to learn to weave. I even have a few old pieces, handwoven here in Appalachia fifty years ago, scattered about the house.

Friends and neighbors spark my interest. When Joyce invites me to a Visitor's Day at nearby Penland School of Crafts, the sight of a loft room filled with about 20 looms threaded with multicolored fibers, yarns and textures rekindles my interest in weaving, and my vision begins to manifest. Jane from Celo Friends Meeting immediately offers me the loan of a small two-harness table loom so I can begin. Nanci cleans up the rusty old loom, figures out how to make the shafts move up and down, and drills holes in the lease sticks. Then Joyce brings me yarn, tools, a warping board, and instructions. Patti is coming over tomorrow to show me how to thread a warp—a community of women supporting me to learn.

In the evenings, I read a book about the intricacies of this new weaving vocabulary—lease stick, sett, epi, reed—and the specifics of measurements and threading the warp. And yet intertwined with these skills is the mystery and beauty of flow, the rhythm of patterns and colors moving up and down and in and out to create a whole fabric of use and beauty.

As I sit with the silence in Friends Meeting this morning, I contemplate how to write this memoir. Weaving is the metaphor that comes to me—a weaving of different strands, balancing warp and weft, color and texture, skill and patience and imagination, to create the whole fabric that is my life.

The root threads of the warp are the constants that hold the tension and support my life as I weave a fabric still in process. The skill is in the balance, maintaining an easeful, steady tension between internal contemplation and outer service, inner seeking and living expression. These warp threads sustain me as I explore the craft of learning to weave.

1
Beaming the Warp

I learn to "beam the warp" on the loom, to fasten the warp threads to the back apron, roll them around the sturdy wood back beam, and then tie them evenly to the front beam. This is the heartwood of weaving—the loom exists to hold the warp yarn ends in even tension, so the weft ends can be woven into them easily. After all the measuring and looping and threading of the yarn, I fasten the ends, in groups of ten or so, to the canvas warp aprons, using square and clove hitch knots. Girl Scout training comes in handy as my hands fumble with tying the knots securely. After I fasten the back ends, the challenge is to tie the front ends evenly, to create a steady tension in the warp. Only now am I ready to begin weaving the weft.

These warp threads hold the weft of my life, rooted securely to the beam of the loom.

Root System

We always call him Father with a capital *F*. He is the oldest of seven, the son of an Episcopal priest from low country South Carolina. Mother is the oldest girl of six, the daughter of a Baptist preacher and farmer from East Texas. There are generations of clergy on both sides of the family, but not until my generation are some of them women–– cousins Janis in Texas and Jennie in South Carolina, and me, the older cousin Jennie. I study family systems in seminary.

~

A closed family system is a tight warp, whose families live in the same place for generations, choosing the same professions and customs. The English/Cornish Bull family arrived in coastal South Carolina in the 1600s, and most live there still. Only World

War II breaks the pattern for the three oldest siblings, who move out of state. My father moves to Texas as an engineer in the war effort, where he meets Mother. Grandmother Bull has a hissy fit when Father marries a nurse from across the Mississippi. Mother never lives down not being a birthright Episcopalian.

The two dispersed oldest cousins maintain the ministerial tradition—with a difference. Peter, now Issachar, is an orthodox rabbi living in Jerusalem, father of twelve children. I, the second oldest, come out as a lesbian, minister in the LGBTQ community, then follow an Indian spiritual path and live in an ashram.

World War II relocates Father from South Carolina to the Dow Chemical plant in Freeport, Texas, where Mother works as a nurse. With 4F status because of mastoid surgery, he had flunked out of University of Pennsylvania medical school. In the 1940s, as the war heats up, Dow Chemical hires him as a chemical engineer and transfers him to its large magnesium plant in Freeport, Texas, making parts for U.S. aircraft, as so many workers migrate across the world. He is the first in his family to leave South Carolina since precolonial times.

~

An open family system is a loose warp, whose members move outward as pioneers and include diverse peoples and cultures. The Scottish Boyds and Irish Splawns also arrive in the 1600s, land in Virginia, migrate to Tennessee, and then on to Texas. Grampy Jim Boyd pastors Baptist churches all over the state, often paid in farm produce, and he manages to put his son and five daughters through college during the Depression. "My girls don't need to have fur coats to go to college." Born and raised in Texas, Mother travels in other ways. First a teacher in one-room schools, she helps to pay for her sisters' college tuition. After she is diagnosed as a diabetic, she defies her mother—"nursing is unladylike"—to study nursing, where she excels, president of her class. She names me after herself and her aunt Jennie, who became the first woman in the family to receive a doctorate.

~

Fate introduces my parents in the Dow plant infirmary, he with painful chlorine burns on his feet from the invisible gas silently seething on the floor of his lab, she nervously cleansing and bandaging his red and blistered feet. He winces as she wipes the antiseptic, winds the bandages, grabs her hand as she supports him to hobble out the door. His lonely pain finds comfort in her gentleness.

He asks her to go horseback riding. They court seated high above the pasture, trot through tall grass, reins loose in their hands. The wedding is in Woodville, the honeymoon on the beachfront in Galveston—in later years when they visit for an anniversary, the hotel has become a nursing home.

In 1942, the U.S. clandestinely constructs the town of Oak Ridge in the mountains of East Tennessee. Father is one of the chemical engineers sent by Dow to produce the Uranium 235 that detonates the atomic bomb to end the war and incinerate Hiroshima and Nagasaki. Mother's sisters Ruth and Lucille come to live with us and work as "Oak Ridge girls" in this then-secretive town with no postal address. After the bomb drops, Father agonizes about his choices and ends up leading ORES, Oak Ridge Engineers and Scientists, which lobbies for civilian control of atomic energy. The FBI follows him for years because of that activist resistance to wartime use of atomic energy. I am born April 23, 1945, the day the Nazi concentration camp Buchenwald is liberated, a child of devastation. My brother John is born two years later. Our family, like thousands of others, is dislocated or destroyed by the war and disease.

Johnny and little Jennie in Oak Ridge, Tennessee, 1947.

When Johnny is six months old and I am two, Mother takes him to the doctor for a checkup because he has nephritis; she diligently nurses him back to health. At the checkup, she is diagnosed with tuberculosis, which means complete bed rest and isolation for six months, through several painful pneumothorax treatments that collapse her lung and create permanent scarring. As a diabetic with TB, she absorbs the pain of war for our family, yet she remains a strong woman who loves and rears her children the best she can. From her I learn courage, to be strong against the odds, a role I play throughout my life, choosing the unfamiliar, risky path to wholeness and community.

The family in crisis, Father decides to attend seminary to become an Episcopal priest like his father before him, and moves Mother, Johnny, and me to Sewanee. He bicycles to class every day, his black academic gown flapping behind him. Our struggling family is supported by the Bishop's Fund, as Father brings home cases of Spam, canned peas, and evaporated milk to feed us. When I get sick and break our household thermometer while I sit shivering by the coal stove, mother scolds me, "Now we have to spend money to buy a new one."

Father teaches me the song for the Hebrew alphabet while he sits in the big armchair in the living room—*"aleph, beth, gimmel, daleth. . . ."* In the back bedroom, Mother takes lots of naps and we have to be quiet. Johnny and I share a bedroom, where I peek at the scary face of a devil woman in a comic book and then hide from her face under the covers each night, as she leers down at me from the corner of the ceiling. During the day, I pass scissors to the girl next door through the crack in the thin wall of the student housing. I learn to swing high with my friend Jeannie, stand tall, my girl's body strong, even if Mother has TB.

~

Under a tall tree on the mountaintop in Sewanee, Jeannie LaValle stands on the wooden seat of the rope swing. I want to swing too—can two of us swing together? Mother and Father, in dress-up clothes, are inside having tea at the professor's house. I just broke one of his wife's teacups. Embarrassed, Mother offered to replace it, but the wife said no. Now I'm playing in the yard; Mother won't see me outside swinging high with Jeannie. I clamber up in my blue overalls, grab the sturdy ropes with both hands, a little unsteady, carefully place my feet on each side of Jeannie, and pull myself up to standing. I've made it! I can stand, even if a bit shaky. I take a deep breath and begin to pump, my sturdy torso pushing us higher and higher, as she pushes too. Soon we swing high in the air, triumphant in a blur of green and blue. I learn the courage to stand in shaky places.

~

Many summers our family vacations on Pawleys Island in coastal South Carolina, where my Bull grandparents live in a rambling old beach rectory, with a wrap-around porch. I love to rock in the big rope hammock at one corner, sweep the dirt through the knothole in the dining room floor, and go crabbing and clamming off the long, planked boardwalk in the stinky saltwater marsh out back. On the ocean side of the porch, brother Johnny and I jiggle on a toggle board, then run over the dunes to play on the beach, splash in the waves, and collect sand dollars, our underpants saggy with sand. As Father and Mother walk back over the dunes from the beach, I run to the edge of the porch and climb up on the rickety wooden railing, scramble to the top, lean over precariously—a towhead smile in my sandy underpants—loving the wind and sand and life. The parents firmly tell me, "Get down, you could fall." I slowly return to the toggle board. All my life, I push the limits with abandon, then heed that internal voice when about to fall—adventure and protection, outbreath and inbreath entwined in steady tension.

Other summers we visit the Boyd farm near Center, Texas. We adopt Eps the turtle, found on the road in Eps, Arkansas, and release him in the farm pond. I get up early to feed the baby chicks with Grampy Jim, set out my cane pole for catfish in the pond, and run under the barbed wire fence to escape the big bull in the pasture. I never learn to hit the garbage can lid with the BB gun when Grampy Jim tries to teach me to shoot. Baptists don't play cards, so in the evenings we play dominoes in the carport while Grandmother shells peas. My earliest memory of overt racism is Grandmother Boyd's scorn and epithet for a Black woman she sees licking an ice cream cone as we drive by the Center town square after Sunday dinner. Embarrassed, I tell my parents, "She shouldn't say that word!" When I sing during a meal, Grandmother reprimands, "Whistling girls and crowing hens always come to no good ends."

~

After Father completes seminary, followed by a brief stay at a church in Nashville, in 1953 we move to Knoxville in East Tennessee, where he serves as rector of St. James Episcopal Church on the edge of town for the next 30 years. The white, lower middle class congregation worships in a simple sanctuary, its beauty in the Connick stained-glass windows.

The blue, red, green, and golden light streams through the stained-glass windows at St. James. The Mary and Martha window shines just above where we always sit, in the third row back on the left, where I ponder its light every Sunday. Martha holds fruit, clothed in green and gold; Mary stands simply, in blue and purple, hands folded in prayer. I love Mary, the woman who chooses to sit at the master's feet, more than Martha who cooks the meal. I weave these two images of woman throughout my life.

~

Father stands in the pulpit preaching, wearing his clerical collar, a black cassock, white surplice, and green stole for Trinity, his face long and dour. He preaches without notes and well; the congregation respects him. Weekdays, he lopes up the steps for lunch, a Pall Mall dangling from his full lips, a tab of cigarette paper stuck to the lower right lip. He's wearing his blue-and-white seersucker suit, jacket over his shoulder, a black shirt with starched white clerical collar, his uniform. Bald and grinning, he both frightens young children and welcomes me with an awkward hug, his breath stiff with tobacco. His long horse face puckers into a whistle as he calls for Mother in the kitchen. Mother whistles her response—their mating call. They kiss, check in, eat lunch, and lie down for a brief nap before he returns to work.

~

Mother stands in the kitchen in her denim wraparound skirt, cotton print blouse, worn brown flats. Her short, curly, light brown hair, soft blue eyes, and round figure complement Father's angularity. A St. Andrews cross is always pinned to her right collar above her breast—her match for his clerical collar. The pastoral couple.

She is the social one—outgoing, empathetic, hardworking. She sews our clothes and cooks our healthful meals and holds the church together emotionally. At the end of a funeral, she takes the hands of two young children. Their mother, her good friend, has died of uterine cancer because the local hospital refused her an abortion. She walks with them down the aisle.

Round and open, she is a bit shy about her 5'10" height. She always wears skirts or dresses and loves big hats. She tells me, "If you can't be beautiful, be charming." She is also a brittle diabetic who takes insulin daily. She suffers several miscarriages and a stillbirth. As a nurse, she carefully maintains her health and ours. As a young child, I learn to watch for the signs of diabetic shock—she begins to giggle and talk a lot. I know how to run to the icebox to bring her a glass of always-handy orange juice. I am the adult child of a diabetic.

Evenings, we drive up to Sharp's Ridge above the city to watch the sun set and the stars come out. If we're lucky, Johnny and I get ice cream cones on the way home. We relax some weekends at a friend's log cabin way up in the foothills of the Smokies, where Johnny and I explore the crawdads in the stream, spiders hiding on the weeds. We scramble up the huge mound of sawdust from the abandoned lumber mill. Sometimes we drive up to the Smokies to swim in the Little Pigeon River, hike to Laurel or Abrams Falls, clamber all the way up to Clingmans Dome. When we climb Mount LeConte, Mother announces, "Children, when you are forty, remember that your mother climbed this mountain." When I'm forty, on a hike to a mountaintop in Colorado during a Boyd family reunion, I remember and share the memory and words of my courageous mother.

~

St. James in Knoxville is my first community. I learn to sing scripture responsively as we chant the psalms in worship, to give nickels and dimes to my mite box and make a weekly pledge, to wash and iron the altar linens. I sing in the junior choir and have a crush on Jane, the church organist. To join the Girl Scout troop at the church, I memorize all four verses of the Star-Spangled Banner. On Sundays after service I visit Patsy or Linda, best friends from church, for dinner and play, returning in the evening for Episcopal Young Churchmen, where supper is always two hamburgers and a coke—twenty-five cents at White Circle. Our family relies on the generosity of church members—the salary is low. I grow up wearing either handsewn or hand-me-down clothes. We wait around on Sunday afternoons for an offer of unused tickets to University of Tennessee football games. I am raised in community, expecting to be cared for in ways that are not in my control.

At twelve, I receive the sacrament of confirmation, wearing a white polished-cotton dress sewn by Mother. I have memorized the catechism: "Who am I? I am a member of Christ, a child of God, and an inheritor of the kingdom of heaven." As the bishop lays hands on my head, I feel warmth pulse from the top of my head down through my body. I know a rush of love and beneficent self-acceptance. The Spirit descends—my first remembered experience of divine indwelling—loved and loveable. While the words and images will change over the years, this truth is a root thread that holds my life steady.

~

Our family becomes an open weave, as the tight warp of our family expands. For the first 14 years of my life, we are big Jen and little Jen, Father John and Johnny. Johnny, two years younger, has big ears that stick out like Grampy Jim's. He delivers newspapers, and I'm the bossy big sister.

Then we adopt Susan when she is ten. While leading a conference on "Christian Family Life" up the mountain near Sewanee, Father calls Mother, asking if she wants to adopt a local girl slated to be sent to the church orphanage in Memphis. That same day, Mother takes us out of school, and we drive up to sit at the head dining table with Father—Christian Family on display. Susan arrives with a cardboard box of clothes; her first act back home is to use my nail polish.

Thanh is an American Field Service exchange student from Vietnam who lives with us in 1963, my senior year in high school. In 1974, when the U.S. pulls out of Vietnam, he sends his pregnant wife Loan and son David on ahead and escapes by helicopter from the roof of the U.S. Embassy in Saigon. Thanh calls my parents from his refugee camp at Fort Chaffee, Arkansas, and they sponsor the family to Knoxville, helping them to make a new home in their new country. Thanh soon gets a job as a civil engineer and Loan sells real estate. Thanh sponsors all eleven of his brothers and sisters to the U.S. and establishes a Buddhist Temple in Knoxville. At Tet, the Vietnamese New Year celebration, Thanh is host and Loan sits

The Bull family in 1963, when Jennie was a high school senior.
Left to right: Susan, Mother, Jennie, Father, John, Thanh.

at the head table wearing elegant jade jewelry. They introduce me as their American sister.

Our open family invites the lonely and grieving for holiday dinners, takes in abused young women as a foster family, invites a young Black couple to hold their wedding in the church, gives food to the "weary world" of the homeless as they trudge to the church office, receives a gun for safe-keeping from an abused wife when she knocks on the door at 2 a.m., bails out the Black Episcopal priest arrested in a civil rights demonstration, buys fifty-cent toys for all our thirty nieces and nephews one Christmas, accepts a lesbian daughter.

~

The house I grew up in smelled like coal and smoke—a grayish yellow grime of acrid smell and taste and film saturating everything. I grew up thinking coal smoke and dust and smell was the way it was—everyone I knew heated their homes this way. We lived in a rectory, the housing the church supplied. The junior warden, who owned a coal company, donated the coal. One year he was angry with my father over a decision at church and delivered a load of soft coal to the house, which when burned, smogged the air and covered all surfaces in thick, smelly coal scum. Mother, Johnny, and I had to wash all the floors and walls and furniture—icky, yucky coal grime. I can see that coal dust on me even now, gray creases in my elbows –and smell those winters in Knoxville, Tennessee—coal country.

~

Seventy years later, I'm still surrounded by smoke. My neighbor Lorena sits at her kitchen table, lights up a Pall Mall, and begins our weekly chat about her dead daughter and how she's cleaning up the back bedroom, everything so covered in tobacco grime. Angels cover the walls of her home—a lifetime collection of porcelain, plastic, china, white, painted, smiling, solemn, flying, standing, embracing angels. The smell of her cigarette stings my nose and sinks into my clothes and skin.

~

Back then, adding to the coal smell were the two and half packs a day Father smoked—first Camels, then Pall Malls, then Marlboro Lights 'til the day he died, after an encapsulated cancer on his lung and quintuple bypass surgery. I'm angry. How come a chain smoker gets to live to be 83 and my mother dies at 63? All that secondhand smoke—coal and tobacco in our skins, clothes, furniture, food, hearts. No angels to protect us, no angels to protect my nurse mother from the diabetes and TB that killed her. I know the weak lungs, deep chest colds, and earaches much of my young life were from the Knoxville coal damp and secondhand fumes. I'm glad I escaped to healthier spaces today.

~

Lorena rarely leaves the house. When she does, she uses her old beat-up metal wheelchair as a walker and grocery cart. She unloads bags of food from the back of her hatchback into the wheelchair, then wheels it up the wooden ramp into her kitchen through the back door, both pushing strongly and leaning heavily for support. She breathes hard to compensate for her overweight body, stiff hips, short breath, fragile heart. She worried when I met her at the back door carrying the watermelon from the car, setting it down with a heavy thud in a cardboard box on the back porch. A retired nurse like my mother, she had an EKG yesterday and is going to the doctor tomorrow, scared of her low energy, afraid for her heart. "I haven't gotten up to make my morning coffee for three days now."

~

The life fires that warm me all have their cost, their crucible burning and even purifying. But those flames don't hold the stagnant, smothering, calcification of black lung, sooty breath, tight chest, clogged hearing of dirty fuels and fumes. How to breathe fresh air, with clean lungs, ears, nose, throat, and sinuses? How to open, expand, see the clear blue sky, know I'm okay? It's more than how a furnace heats a house.

Is this all learning for when my time comes? What will I push one day to get the groceries into the house? One of the last times I visited Father before he died, I told him I wouldn't stay inside with him when he smoked, so we took a walk. Lorena, my kind neighbor, I'll keep checking in on you. May all your angels protect us both.

2
Warp Threads

Mother goes all out on my seventh birthday in 1952, choosing a cowgirl theme because I like to watch Roy Rogers and Dale Evans on our new TV—"Happy trails to you, until we meet again." She sends my friends a colorful invitation with a cowgirl on a pony throwing a lasso that circles the invite. She bakes a cake with dotted red cherry notes on the icing, the melody of "Happy Birthday to You." Using the old Singer treadle machine with the chain stitch that unravels when you pull it, she sews a cowgirl skirt and vest of blue denim, its seams zigzagged with pinking shears to look like fringe.

I'm embarrassed by the cowgirl outfit because the zigzag seams are on the outside—it's wrong side out! Reluctantly, I put on the skirt and vest and stand on the front porch by myself, uncertain. I'm afraid to wear this outfit to play in the neighborhood. What will Ann Lillard say, the loud girl who has the first TV on the block? I will not wear it to school, for sure. Do I want to be a cowgirl anyway? What *do* I want to be? Mother says I can be anything I want to be when I grow up.

~

The warp threads knot tightly in place by my East Tennessee roots: Southern lady grandmothers from east Texas and coastal South Carolina; light through stained glass windows in the Episcopal church where Father is rector; family hikes to waterfalls in the Smokies; me a sixth-grade champion speller and reader of *all* the children's biographies in the library. I'm a white, lower middle-class girl in conservative, sixty percent Southern Baptist, segregated Knoxville, Tennessee. Father counsels me, "You're going to college for a liberal arts education, so you can be a good wife to your future husband." I tell Mother, "When I grow up,

I want to be married to a minister and sit around and read all the time."

I don't fit the Southern lady frame. How to expand this narrow warp?

Education is the thread. I apply to Swarthmore College—definitely not a Southern school—and in 1963 attend on full scholarship. I'm ecstatic at my choices—to walk in the woods of the campus arboretum, view classic art films, folk dance under the stars, write literary critiques, and open to the world of European ideas of men and literature. My favorite poem is T.S. Eliot's "Four Quartets." Swarthmore is a Quaker school in the 1960s. I learn for the first time that faith can call one to social action. I attend my first civil rights march in nearby Chester, Pennsylvania, and protest the war in Vietnam, all in protected, white, upper-class suburban Philadelphia.

~

In the 1960s, Black Power leaders ask white activists to work with white folks. After graduation in 1967, I return to the Appalachian Mountains as a volunteer with the American Friends Service Committee, where I choose to continue my education in the War on Poverty. I was all set to give out medications to TB patients in the slums of Madras, but the Indian government was granting visas to agriculture experts and engineers that year, not English majors, so I ended up teaching General Education classes with the Neighborhood Youth Corps in Hazard, Kentucky.

Neighborhood Youth Corps classes are mandatory one day a week for General Education students, kids 18 to 22 who have not gone past the eighth grade and thus are ineligible for the more frequent GED classes for other Youth Corps kids. The students are assigned make-work jobs like cleaning the courthouse in return for their small stipend. The kids in the classes are married, jobless, barely literate, younger than I am but much older in life experience. They don't want to be here in this class.

I learn about mountain crafts—pottery, quilts, weaving—and fall in love with Howard, a Philadelphia Quaker and former classmate who volunteered with AFSC in Vietnam. Having learned well to please with hand-sewn creations, I design and stitch a red-and-yellow calico quilt for my boyfriend, knit a shawl for his sister, and embroider a skirt for his mother one Christmas.

It's the height of the U.S. war in Vietnam and the year of King's assassination in 1968. The students in the Youth Corps class are restless, and I am angry. Some of them have never seen a Black person. Martin Luther King Jr. was murdered yesterday. I stand in front of their desks and ask them to write about the news and their response. I walk past two boys in the back, sitting at battered wooden desks with initials carved over the dark, oil-stained surface. I see stick figures of a man hanging by a noose

Jennie at the Pine Mountain Settlement School, Kentucky, 1968.

from a tree. I grab the offensive drawings from the two guys, stride to the front of the room, and angrily announce, "Reverend Martin Luther King was a great man, so respect him." My hands shake, my voice trembles, and I'm close to tears. The guys in the back look down, sullen. I agonize, cry, write anguished letters to other volunteers. I can't stand to live and teach in this bigoted town, when U.S. cities are aflame and rage is erupting. I want to be where the action is.

I move to Washington, DC, to live with Howard. I teach classes to Black and Latino Youth Corps students who work at the Catholic University cafeteria to earn their stipend. We live in Norman Morrison House, a Quaker commune near 14th Street in Washington, DC—a plantation city of white-columned edifices built by enslaved African Americans. Again, I'm ignorant of the lives around me.

When we marry in 1969, Mother sews my dress from cloth woven in Berea, Kentucky, with a pale blue border in a traditional mountain pattern. It is beautiful, and still I resist the Southern lady role. The night before our Pendle Hill wedding, Howard sleeps with the man who bakes our wedding cake—a harbinger of our future that I ignore. I kick off my shoes and skip barefoot through the grass as we folk dance at the wedding. We twist clover into soon-to-wilt wedding rings, donate most of the wedding gifts to Goodwill, and buy a used sewing machine with wedding money. I sew voluminous flowery shifts and head scarves for myself and soon enough find opportunities for activism.

~

After my arrest for civil disobedience, the guard in the DC jail searches my body roughly when I descend from the paddy wagon into the tiny room. She commands me to undress, turn around, and bend over to see if I'm concealing anything. She wants to take my contact lenses so they won't be stolen. I refuse to hand them over, more afraid of blindness than theft in this strange place.

The heavy metal door closes with a clank that echoes along the concrete halls as I enter the Cloroxed holding cell. The women in green jumpsuits sit on bunk beds, protesting the johns who ratted on them and sharing desperate tales of the world of prostitution. I sit silently on the edge of a bed and eat the food on the tray—white bread and beans pasty in my mouth. I'm intimidated by their bravado and tough lives and finally will myself to sleep, exhausted, clutching my lens case.

Hours earlier, I stood on the white marble steps of the U.S. Capitol building with Quakers and read the names of American soldiers who died in Vietnam—feeling courageous and righteous in my homemade shift and scarf. It's my first act of civil disobedience. One by one, the cops lead us away, and my parents see it all on national news in Knoxville. The next morning in court, the judge throws out our arrests; there is no law against peaceful assembly on the steps of the U.S. Capitol. Congress passes one shortly afterwards.

The warp colors and patterns expand.

3
Women's Warp

Toad Hall, the Quaker commune in Baltimore where Howard and I live in 1970, is a brick, three-story row house on Calvert Street in Charles Village, near Johns Hopkins University. The eight of us—three women and five men—renovate the house for reduced rent, cook and eat vegetarian dinners with chopsticks, and sit on cushions around a low table-door. We listen to Janis Joplin and Moody Blues, experiment with dope, and listen to tapes of a Guru from India. We are four blocks away from Waverly, the racially mixed working-class neighborhood along Greenmount Avenue.

I begin to attend the new weekly women's consciousness-raising meetings in Waverly. While sitting in a circle, we take turns sharing our anger and experiences as women. We are mostly white, middle class, married, college educated, and unemployed; several have young children. In 1969, Donna, Vicki, DeeAnn, and Carmen had formed a collective to publish *Women: A Journal of Liberation*, one of the first feminist periodicals. The Journal office occupies one room upstairs at the People's Free Medical Clinic on Greenmount Avenue. The clinic, begun in the late 1960s by a group of leftist men, including Howard—many of them the husbands of these feminists—offers free medical care to its neighbors and welcome space for progressive community events. The large room upstairs in the back is the site of the first women's dances in Baltimore, in the early 1970s—jubilant liberation to dance freely with other women. In 1974, around the corner and down the block on 31st Street, next to the Belly food coop and across from the Bread and Roses coffeehouse, some of these same women inaugurate the 31st Street Bookstore, which continues for 21 years as a feminist collective until 1994. This

Winter 1971 *Women: A Journal*.
Cover by Linda Carpenter.

one-square block of Baltimore holds the story of much of my life in Baltimore. It is a neighborhood to which I'll return over ten years later, an important thread in the warp.

~

I sit cross-legged in a circle on the floor of the small upstairs Journal office, facing the sunny street-side window, along with the rest of the Journal collective—Donna, Karen, Vicky, DeeAnn, Carmen, Emilie, Valentine, Jeannie. A stack of dark brown, heavy cardboard mail slots towers behind me, where we stuff papers by subject for each issue, our only file system. A couple of small desks and typewriters, an easel, and posters line the walls of the room, but little else. The focus is on our twice-weekly collective meetings, where we plan the theme, write the editorial, and select the content of upcoming issues—color cover, 80 b&w ad-free pages, five issues for $5/year. As one of the first national feminist journals, we are consciously creating feminist ideology, poetry, and art, networking with women's groups around the country and reporting on their activities. We spend many long hours developing the lead editorial based on the theme for each issue: "Inherent Nature or Cultural Conditioning?" "What is Liberation?" "Women in History: A Re-creation of our Past," "Women and Revolution," "The Image of Women in the Arts."

At today's meeting, we discuss the editorial and content for "What is Liberation?" The founders consider themselves socialist feminists, so the tone of the editorial is intellectual—we use words like "alienation," "dialectic," and "material conditions." The much more visceral articles, photos, and art come from the lives and experiences of the contributors: "The Politics of Day Care," "Twelve and Turned On," "Building Extended Families." The twenty-plus pages of the Movement Section at the back vibrate with letters, events, publications, buttons, abortion info, and a guide to feminist activities in cities across the country and globally: "Women attack ROTC in Seattle and Ithaca," "Redstockings," "Daughters of Bilitis."

The subheadings of this Liberation issue are birth control, families and day care, education, jobs, and self-defense. I contribute an article for the education section on "High School Women: Oppression and Liberation," writing about my experience as an organizer of the Quaker AFSC Learning Action Center free school project with Howard, who goes on to head the first alternative high school in Baltimore. I focus on the rigid social expectations of young women in high school. As they rebel, our center offers safe space to explore alternatives to gender roles and indoctrination. Lesbianism and gender identity are not part of the conversation in 1969 and not part of my vocabulary yet, either. I ask, "Is it okay that Howard took the photos of two young Baltimore women who illustrate my article? Shouldn't a woman's photography be used?"

I'm new in town, so want to learn how to participate in this Journal collective. What can I do to support it? The subscription service and newsstand distribution are contracted out, but someone needs to come to the Journal office between meetings to receive and categorize all the submissions—articles, photos, art, and poetry mailed in by women for each issue. (No email or computers back then.) I soon volunteer for and become the first paid staff at the Journal—part-time and rewarding. I love sorting through the mail, the letters and contributions from women around the country who, like us in Baltimore, are wakening to this wave of feminism. I learn by reading, organizing, and stuffing papers into different cardboard cubbyholes for each issue. I soon combine and present thematic groupings of art and poetry and articles for intense discussion and selection at our meetings. Which poem goes with which drawing and with which article?

Slowly, I begin to contribute my own voice to the fiery conversations about privilege, conditioning, and inequalities. With my long, dark hair and home-sewn cotton shifts, how can I unlearn all the "good girl" conditioning of my growing up? I've stopped wearing makeup and a bra, but do I want to stop shaving the dark hair on my legs and under my arms? That feels too risky.

The men at Toad Hall are beginning to experiment with sex, and I'm hurt when Howard sleeps with another woman. I refuse to experiment with him, begin to raise feminist issues in the commune, and patiently try to "educate" the men. As I withdraw, my anger builds.

Feminism is now part of the weave, and the warp shifts. In December 1971, I leave Howard and the Toad Hall commune, move into the first women's collective in Baltimore, and come out as a lesbian, all by the end of 1972. When I announce at a

Journal meeting that I'm lesbian, I'm greeted with shocked silence; everyone else is married or straight. My presence is threatening—I soon leave. Howard ends up marrying one of the other Journal women.

~

We decide to name our brave new women's collective after Ida Brayman, a 17-year-old Ukrainian Jewish garment worker killed while on strike for better working conditions in Rochester, New York, in 1913. We rent a duplex two-story frame house on Gorsuch, a side street in the working-class neighborhood of Waverly, just off Greenmount Avenue and the People's Free Medical Clinic and east of more upscale Charles Village and Toad Hall. We make a class and racial shift in the move, part of the emerging leftist and feminist hub in Baltimore in the 1970s. A group of leftist men live in a commune down the street, and together we plan political actions and war resistance and found a local food coop. The one Black woman in their commune runs the food coop. We call ourselves socialist feminists.

Carmen, Susan, Casey, Ann, Gretchen, and I are the first members of Ida Brayman—one Latina, one working-class Detroit woman, two middle class Baltimore Jewish women, and Southern middle-class me. Casey, Carmen, and Susan decide to make a vegetable garden in the side lot along the house. Casey dumps a truckload of manure for compost, which stinks up the neighborhood. We paint the Vietnamese NFL flag on the living room floor, in bold red and blue with yellow star. We dance to Roberta Flack and Carol King and smoke dope. None of us have jobs. I embroider women's symbol patches and sew them on the seat and knees of my jeans.

I develop a crush on Casey from Detroit, working class, artist, lover of horses. Her main attraction for me is her participation in the 1969 Women Against Daddy Warbucks draft board action in New York. She and four other women raided Manhattan draft boards overnight and destroyed most of the 1-A files, then appeared the next day at Rockefeller Center to toss the shredded files into the air. I want to be a committed and savvy revolutionary like her.

We all sleep in that upstairs middle bedroom, the mattress room. Six thin single mattresses with heavy, musty gray cotton ticking cover the floor, piled with sleeping bags or a tangle of

Women of Ida Brayman collective in our garden, 1972.
Left to right: Jennie, Casey, Susan, Carmen, Greta,
and neighborhood children.

sheets and blankets. Along the back wall, we each stash our clothes in cardboard boxes, open on the side. We store our other possessions in the front bedroom where Ann chooses to sleep alone.

I usually sleep in the middle of the mattress room next to Casey, breathing carefully, so wanting to touch her, the sexual tension gradually building. Some nights I don't sleep at all, managing to carefully edge my thigh over to touch hers, feeling the warmth of a woman's skin against mine.

That crucible year, we slowly begin to sort ourselves out. We begin to abandon the mattress room and sleep in separate rooms, as some come out and others leave.

To my dismay, Casey gets together with Coletta, a lesbian mother and member of the radical Furies collective in DC, and she moves into a house across the street with Coletta, Chris, and Sarina. Ann connects with Citti, who studies Greek so she can translate Sappho's poetry. Susan never finds her place, after trying to indoctrinate us into her housekeeping ways. I do not wash dishes the way she wants me to. I'm supposed to put some liquid detergent on the sponge, wash the dish, then rinse it—not put the detergent in the water.

Casey and Coletta, Chris and Sarina, Ann and Citti and I found Diana Press, renting a basement storefront on 25th Street, closer to downtown. Diana publishes *Songs to a Handsome Woman*, Rita Mae Brown's first poetry chapbook. We have serious conflicts with the Furies collective, the "cultural feminists" in Washington, DC, who are separatists and publish *Quest, a Feminist Quarterly*. Casey and Coletta continue the press when it moves to California in 1974.

"Women-identified women" is the topic when Rita Mae visits Baltimore to meet with Diana Press. She is the first out lesbian I've ever met. I'm tongue-tied and awkward and follow her around like a puppy dog, listening to every word. One statement stays with me, "I want to live my life on the cutting edge of history, so lesbians after me will have a better life." That sounds right to me, and I soon announce I'm a lesbian, cut my long hair, stop shaving my legs, and begin taking Tae Kwon Do classes twice a week to strengthen my body and release my anger. I come out to my parents in a letter home. They quickly drive north for an awkward visit, distressed but cautiously accepting. Father asks why I've cut my long hair. Mother has a hard time, says lesbianism is "unnatural." I explain to her that some folks are right-handed and some are left-handed—a minority but still natural—and that's how it is with me. She bites her lip and doesn't argue.

~

During a rowdy anti-Vietnam War demonstration in downtown Baltimore, I'm arrested again, and this time sentenced to probation and a $1,000 fine. To pay, I take a job as a proofreader and pasteup artist at Ad Design across town. I'm middle class, the only one with a full-time job, taking the bus or carpooling to work to punch the time clock, and using my paycheck for Tae Kwon Do classes downtown. The other women pressure me to share more of my money, but I'm unwilling to give up what's needed to pay for the karate lessons—I already put extra in the money jar in the front room. "You're too middle class," asserts Coletta, and the tension begins to build.

We drive downtown to Mitch's lesbian bar on weekends, where Mitch and Ricky run the only watering hole for white lesbians in Baltimore. I never learn to play pool, though I do try out the dyke softball games and touch football on Sunday afternoons, led by Mitch, but feel inadequate and clumsy.

One evening at Mitch's, I meet Chris, a working-class dyke, and soon she moves in across the street with Casey and Coletta. Chris comes on to me, offers to "bring me out" sexually. She is strong and vulnerable, loves her dog Lady, has soft hands. I come out in a back bedroom at Ida Brayman when Chris makes love to me for the first time. I'm in love—mystified and hurt when Chris breaks up with me after three months, succumbing to the class tension from Coletta.

Devastated by the breakup with Chris, I move out of Ida Brayman into a tiny one-room attic apartment with sloping ceilings just a block up the street on Gorsuch. I adopt Pooka, a white Manx cat, and begin to learn what it means to live on my own in this new lesbian world. I contribute to *The Palm of Your Hand*, a book of poetry by Baltimore lesbians. "This witch and her witchy Pooka cat are putting a spell on you."

~

Women's self-defense is one of the themes of the Journal issue on Liberation, as feminists literally begin to fight back. I've never been athletic, other than hiking in the mountains growing up, and want to feel my power as a woman. Mother was physically weak, and my parents never encouraged me to develop physical skills. I grew up before Title IX legislated equal physical education for women in 1972. Fulton High School had no team sports for women, and I got through Swarthmore with only the minimal PE requirements—walks in the woods and folk dancing my only exercise. So Tae Kwon Do classes were the beginning of a lifelong journey to integrate mind and body, get out of my head, use my body to express my feelings and claim my power, and come out as a whole woman.

I resolve to grow strong and enroll in twice-weekly classes in Tae Kwon Do, a Korean martial art that focuses on fast jumping and spinning kicks and punches. The studio is on the second floor of a downtown office building in Baltimore, across

Diana Press dykes in 1972:
Back, left to right: Casey, Delores, Chris. *Front:* Coletta, Lee, Jennie.

from the main Enoch Pratt Library, with wide, floor-to-ceiling windows that illumine our practice space.

    I invest in a white cotton karate outfit of pants, kimono-style jacket with long sleeves, and white belt. Mr. Park, the Korean teacher, and his wife, a young American woman and senior instructor, lead the formal classes. Almost all the students are men. Every few months Park conducts a performance exam and posts the names of students who pass on the bulletin board, indicating the belt color they may now wear: it's white for beginners, then yellow, green, blue, brown, and the coveted black belt. Over the next two years, I gradually move from white to yellow to green belt.

    I learn a grounded stance, to move from my waist, and gradually begin to develop strength in my thighs and core. We practice lots of push-ups and sit-ups, learn to punch with clenched fist, hit punching bags, and practice kicks with those same bags—side kick, back kick, front kick, sweep kick. Soon I'm sparring with a partner and learning to pull the punches and kicks—self-control while responding to the other person's attack. The men leave us alone and I work with the other women, grateful for the woman assistant.

On the day of my test for the blue belt, Park spars with me directly and immediately trips me down to the ground, ready to punch my face, his eyes glaring down at me. I'll never forget those fierce eyes and what they taught me about how much more I had to learn. I never made blue belt.

My final triumph comes when Park takes us to a demonstration to perform one of the *katas*, or forms. Then, unexpectedly, he brings out a 2x4 board, sets it at waist level held by two students, and asks each of us to throw a kick to break the board. I've never seen or tried this in my life—no YouTube videos back then—and the first two times I miss. Park looks at me and says, "One more chance." I breathe deep, kick, and break the board—Crack!

With Lee from the Furies in DC and Casey, we initiate a women's Tae Kwon Do class in Baltimore, practicing in a gym at Johns Hopkins University. Even with my minimal knowledge of the martial art, I know many women want to strengthen their bodies and self-confidence. Once a week, we gather to march up and down the floor with kicks and punches, yelling with our breath. I begin to understand how important this discipline is for me in releasing all the anger and tension from my coming out and feminist rage. I love to work up a sweat. I teach what I know.

As anger releases and confidence builds, my physical practice evolves over the years into the gentler, more internal style of Tai Chi Chuan and Qigong, which I teach today. But its root thread began years ago in that early feminist year of coming out and wanting to be strong.

In 1972, warp threads stretch tight, revolution is my religion, and the fabric of the women's community frays in class and race and sexual conflict. I'm on the edge of snapping—how to keep my life and heart in one piece? I choose to hold the warp steady, to strengthen and secure the weave before it breaks.

4
Rainbow Weft

Settled into my attic apartment with Pooka the white Manx as companion, I begin to weave my life as a lesbian. I buy a used VW Beetle, my first car, land a job as managing editor at *Turf and Sport Digest*, a monthly Thoroughbred racing magazine, and outsource its typesetting to Diana Press, run by my lesbian friends.

Life in the lesbian community in Baltimore in the early 1970s is centered around butch and femme roles, around mostly white, working-class dykes who have been out for a while. I wonder where the Black lesbians hang out in this segregated city. We gather on weekends at Mitch's bar for dancing, pool, and touch football, sustained by weekend binges of drinking before returning to a work week in the suffocating closet. Living "in the closet" isolates, requires avoiding references to home life and family, what matters most. We learn to lie habitually, replace "we" with "I."

What did you do over the holidays?

Lie: "Nothing much; just visited the folks."

Truth: "My parents won't let my lover visit and we've celebrated Christmas separately for the past five years—I'm constantly torn between her and family."

Then there are the baby dykes, including me, who are mostly white middle-class feminists, newly out, politically active, and seeking safe space to love and meet one another. We are awed by the swagger of the butches and a bit disdainful of the femmes in their makeup and nail polish.

Sylvia "Sibbie" Deal arrives at Mitch's bar one evening in 1973 and begins to attend lesbian events. A white dyke in her thirties, Sibbie dresses in slacks and turtlenecks and smokes

Marlboros. She lives in a small tract house in Landover, a mixed race, working-class suburb of Washington, DC, an hour away. Sibbie is one of the few people I know who was born and raised in the District of Columbia, and therefore has never voted. She runs a mainframe computer with punch cards at a local diaper service. She has recently stopped drinking and drives the hour to Baltimore on weekends in search of community after her complex triangle of relationships has dissolved. And there I am, waiting to pursue and be pursued, wanting some stability and security in my life. Sibbie is honest and kind. She visits my tiny attic apartment when I'm miserable with a cold and loves me anyway. I choose the only lesbian I know who owns a house and a car and has a steady job, fall in love with her strong, vulnerable self, and move to Landover, an hour away from work.

In 1974, I take an editorial job at Preservation Press, with the National Trust for Historic Preservation, just off Lafayette Square near the White House. The new job requires that I invest in "downtown clothes," so I tie a scarf around my neck and take the new subway to work each day. I don't want to be closeted at work, so resolve to "come out," swallow my fear, and at the interview tell the boss I'm lesbian. She hires me anyway.

Thus begins the weft weave of professional work with words. Having survived the fraying edges of revolutionary politics and heartbreak, it's time to integrate the threads of this wild coming out into a sustainable weave of home and work.

~

I long for some form of spiritual community and find it in Metropolitan Community Church (MCC). After we've been together for a few months, Sibbie and I seek public acknowledgment of our relationship, a spiritual blessing of our love. We hear about MCC, a church in DC that offers ceremonies for same sex couples. Hedging, we decide on a Rite of Blessing instead of the commitment implied in a Holy Union. We both wear dark slacks, turtlenecks, and plaid jackets. We exchange braided silver rings at the ceremony in the chapel of First Congregational Church downtown, where MCC-DC worships and rents office space. That evening, we parade down the streets with lesbian friends, jubilant. I've come out as a lesbian, affirmed my love, and now find myself drawn into a church of mostly white gay men, a

Sibbie and Jennie at their MCC Rite of Blessing in 1973.
Photo by Sharon Deevey.

feminist activist within patriarchal Christianity, confronting the tight warp of my past.

~

Metropolitan Community Church is an ecumenical, international denomination with a socially active ministry in the lesbian and gay community, including trans and bisexual folks. It was founded by Troy Perry, a gay defrocked Pentecostal minister, in 1968 in California, one year before the Stonewall riots. In his autobiography, *The Lord Is My Shepherd and Knows I'm Gay*, Perry recounts the early years of the denomination's active outreach for human rights for all people, affirming lesbian and gay relationships, and providing a safe space and support for those in the community who have internalized years of homophobic exclusion and damnation from most of mainstream Christianity. Today, over 50 years later, MCC has grown to 300 congregations in 22 countries, under the leadership of Nancy Wilson from 2005 to 2016. Half of all MCC clergy are now women and many are people of color.

~

Sibbie's two-bedroom house in Landover sits on a side street in a row of tract houses with white aluminum siding and shutters, just off the Baltimore-Washington Parkway in Prince George's County. My main focus is learning the routines of housekeeping after living communally for years and learning to live with a smoker and a newly recovering alcoholic who does not attend Alcoholics Anonymous. I'm her *de facto* recovery support, which involves hours of deep listening to her often profound intuitions and yearnings. Sometimes I cope with sporadic days of withdrawn silence.

Sibbie lives with and cares for her sister Ida, two years younger, who has Downs Syndrome. Ida attends a sheltered workshop during the day and helps with our weekly housecleaning on the weekends. She speaks clearly, cannot read or write, is overweight and deeply intuitive. Ida gradually draws me out of my bookish head to listen more deeply to feelings, mine and hers. When I'm hurting about a clash with Sibbie, Ida comes to sit beside me, puts her soft hand on the back of my neck, and gently strokes away the anger and tension. And yet I wrestle with guilt and resentment at Sibbie's protectiveness of Ida. I want privacy and eventually convince Sibbie to build an extra bedroom for the two of us on the back of the house, barely large enough for bed and dresser, yet welcome space.

Class tensions come up soon enough in our relationship. As an educated woman, I encourage Sibbie to go to college while I support the household. She quits work and attends Prince George's Community College, the first in her family. I spend hours helping her to write assigned papers. As we sit on the sofa in the evenings, I routinely review and edit drafts of her homework, which I later realize is too enabling. When exam time comes, Sibbie is on her own. It takes three anxious tries for her to pass the required final tests. I'm relieved as she finally makes it. We celebrate the proud graduate.

~

In MCC I learn to loosen up, to worship with my whole body, to clap and sway when I sing, to pray from the heart instead of *The Book of Common Prayer*. The worship experience is powerful—we sing in heartfelt gratitude for our reclaimed faith, we receive open communion as couples, we hold one another in prayer. And it's here that I fight the inclusive language wars, move beyond my internalized childhood image of God the Father—literally Father in the pulpit—to a more inclusive understanding and language for the divine within and around me. I work from the outside in, determined that the language will reflect my reality as a woman. First, I remove all verbal references to God as Father and He from my speaking and begin to use more generic terms and feminine words and images. Then I use Wite-Out to change words in the hymnal, fill my Bible with penciled revisions of scripture, and seek out biblical stories about women—Mary and Martha reappear from the stained-glass window of my childhood at St. James in Knoxville.

I've been behind the scenes with spiritual authority figures all my life, so I fight this good fight with Larry, the pastor, develop a strong love/hate bond with him, often use him as a male punching bag against which I define my own spirituality. I both fight to free myself from the hold of Father in my life and continue the family tradition by becoming student clergy. In 1978 I apply to attend seminary and I convince Sibbie to support me. We've lived off my editor's paycheck while she's in school, and now it's my turn; she returns to her job at the mainframe computer.

I am the first out lesbian admitted to Wesley Theological Seminary, a United Methodist school affiliated with American University, and attend on full scholarship, my very presence a political statement, especially in my first class—on sexuality in the Christian tradition. I self-publish an anthology, *Feminist Views of Christianity*, reprinting articles by Rosemary Radford Ruether, Mary Daly, and other feminist theologians. One of my professors assigns the book for a class. In theology class, I write a paper on the Trinity, the divine as Speaker, Word, and Voice —creative, embodied, breathing presence—both immanent and transcendent, an understanding that continues to support me today. After an intern year, I receive my M.Div. in 1982, summa cum laude, and the Social Ethics award. Rowdy lesbian friends

Jennie's ordination as MCC clergy in 1983. *Left to right:* Troy Perry, Jennie Boyd Bull, Nancy Wilson, Delores Berry, Larry Uhrig.

cheer when I cross the stage at graduation. Father flies up from Knoxville to attend.

I follow the family tradition, though as a woman and a lesbian who claims the divine within me. I feel like I'm radically changing history in my very body; the transformation takes years, goes deep, and is painful in ways I've yet to know.

~

The year I begin seminary is the year Mother dies of a sudden, massive stroke at age 63. Ten years ago, she lost a lobe of her lung—recurrent TB exacerbated by scars from the many pneumothorax treatments she received while I was a toddler. The month before her death, I wrote her a letter about my decision to go to seminary. She responded warmly—"You stretch my soul"—this mother who had such a hard time accepting my life as a lesbian, yet steadily opened her heart to me.

She and Father had just put Grandmother Bull on a plane home to Charleston, South Carolina, after a visit, always tension filled. Father lit up one of his Marlboro Lights in the car, and Mother was dead of a stroke within hours. Sibbie and I flew to Knoxville, the family gathered, and we grieved. I was only 33 and she was so young.

Her early death changes my life. I've always been a daddy's girl. Throughout my adolescence I resisted Mother and disdained the woman's roles they sought to teach me. Now, my unraveling of Father God interweaves with an inner and outer journey to deepen knowledge of myself as a woman and reclaim the Mother threads in me. I begin using Mother's maiden name as my middle name, Boyd, and become Jennie Boyd Bull. I attend Boyd family reunions in Texas, get to know my Boyd aunts and cousins. I undertake the long challenge of consciously interweaving body and mind and heart, of weaving together the mind-body split I have lived all my life.

~

As a church welcoming people from all religious backgrounds, MCC is truly a rainbow community, with the resulting struggles around unity—men and women and in between, white and Black, Catholic and Baptist, liturgical and Pentecostal, fundamentalist and Unitarian, middle and working class, butches and drag queens. Although the DC congregation is majority middle-class white gay men, it also includes many struggling folk—Black, white, and Latinx—who have fled violence and rejection in more rural communities. In our very bodies and loves, worshipping together at MCC forces us to integrate sexuality with spirituality. Couples receive communion together, march with an MCC banner in the Gay Pride parade and lobby for a DC human rights ordinance, bring parents to worship. In Bible study and sermons, we confront centuries of homophobic interpretation of scripture and institutional exclusion. We find the inner and collective courage to witness to the varied textures of love.

The gay men in the church resist mightily when I'm appointed to the denominational Inclusive Language task force, charged to revise the language in the statement of faith. During the 1976 MCC General Conference, our feminist group places copies of a new hymn on the pews, to sing during worship—it eventually becomes an MCC favorite:

Our God is not a woman, our God is not a man,
Our God is both and neither, our God is I who Am.
From all the roles that bind us our God has set us free.
What freedom does God give us? The freedom just to be.

~

It's 1980, and I'm the new Minister of Outreach at Metropolitan Community Church in Washington, DC. As I complete my final, intern year at Wesley Seminary, I'm newly licensed clergy and now wear a white tab collar with a colorful array of clerical shirts. My favorite is blue. What does it mean to use the title Reverend with my name? I have my own desk now in the office with Frank, the assistant pastor, down the hall from pastor Larry. I preach occasionally, but mostly my job is to reach out beyond this congregation of gay white men. What does Minister of Outreach mean here at MCC-DC, a congregation renting office and worship space from the United Church of Christ in the heart of downtown DC?

It means outreach to lesbians. My first step is to organize a small weekly discussion group for lesbians in the church and focus on offering support, building community. I also reach out into the wider lesbian and gay community. Gay is what we call ourselves back then, but I insist on adding lesbian. Trans and bisexual queers are also with us—LGBTQ doesn't appear until the 1990s. DC is one of the landing spots for lesbians and gays who are kicked out of, or escape from, more rural areas and run to the city. Too many end up desperate, on the streets. MCC is one of the area's only free counseling options for lesbians and gays, so I list myself with the city's Lesbian Resource and Counseling Center—and listen. I get to know the Whitman-Walker Clinic, Frank Kameny and other longtime political leaders, and end up appointed to the DC Human Rights Commission—their token lesbian as we lobby for a gay rights ordinance in DC.

I also outreach to the suburbs. A small group of gays and lesbians led by Ken want to start a church in Fairfax, a Virginia suburb of DC. I'm assigned to establish the congregation. Ken is a tough cookie, insists that he is the leader and resists this woman intruder from DC. We rent space from the Unitarian Church in Fairfax and begin meeting for worship on Sunday afternoons in the round, open-space, glass-walled sanctuary in the woods, folding chairs arranged in a semicircle. I wear an off-white linen robe with colorful stole for the season, preach and celebrate communion each Sunday, get to know folks. The congregation is both gay and lesbian, mostly white and middle class, a few interracial couples. Within a year, MCC licenses us as a mission. I work with them, over Ken's objections, to call their own pastor. Their parting gift to me is a large painting of two Siamese cats, which they all sign on the back. "Thank you for all your concern and caring during my hour of need." It hangs in my home to this day.

And then there is outreach in the neighborhood of the church in DC, next to the library, where many homeless folks hang out during the day. The Lutheran church a few blocks over converts its basement into a shelter for homeless women at night, and I begin to volunteer on Tuesdays, listening to their anguished nightmare cries, steeped in the stink of urine and sweat and desperation. I persuade the men in the church to offer their cooking skills to prep large pans of macaroni and cheese, pizza, scalloped potatoes, stew, and cornbread for the thirty or so women who line up outside the back door of the church three evenings a week. We call ourselves the Dinner Program for Homeless Women, an effort with other downtown churches to respond to the homeless mentally ill released to live on the streets. Ruth and Jody are a homeless lesbian couple who eat with us and sleep in the shelter. They give me a cut glass, brass doorknob they found somewhere. I've used it as a paperweight at my desk for years, a reminder that everyone has something to give.

Outreach takes many forms, many directions, all expanding beyond the gay culture that is the norm at the church. I reach out to create my new home and role. As always, bring diverse communities together, expanding my understanding of who I am, as I weave myself into the life of the community:

- I march with rainbow banners in LGBTQ parades and demonstrations, including as a protesting voice in the first Washington for Jesus march by the conservative Christian Right in 1980, carrying a sign "I am a lesbian and Jesus is my Lord;"
- I support MCC in sponsoring gay men from Cuba, prisoners released by Castro as refugees in the Mariel Boatlift of 1980;
- I edit and publish the church newsletter for years, using my writing skills;
- I perform a Rite of Blessing for Rita Mae Brown and Martina Navratilova, who fly me to their country home in Virginia, where I officiate at a private ceremony under the big oak trees on their expansive front lawn, followed by lunch at the country club.

~

The reality of being an out lesbian minister confronts the homophobia in my partner Sibbie's family in a way that tears at our relationship. A Northern Virginia newspaper runs an article about our new MCC congregation in Fairfax, along with a photo of me wearing a white robe with a colorful rainbow stole draped across my body, following the family tradition, lesbian-style. We are ecstatic about the publicity until Sibbie's evangelical relatives see the article and sound the alarm about her sister Ida attending MCC. They sue to take custody of Ida away from Sibbie. Ida takes the stand in court. When asked about her experience at MCC, she testifies, "Jesus is there." The family loses the case and Ida stays with Sibbie, but the damage with her family remains.

The relationship with Sibbie wears thin and frays as I grow more self-aware. I test myself physically to break out of the homebody rut by signing up for the 50-mile Survival Challenge, an overnight hike along the Potomac C&O canal towpath from Ellicott City to Georgetown, training for several weeks. I've been walking all night and am low energy that morning, as I arrive at the mile 40 resting place, hours later than planned. I'm disappointed to see Sibbie and Ida waiting for me. It's the time I asked them to pick me up, but I still have ten miles to go and want to complete the walk. I choose to stop so they won't have to wait. I resent falling short and feel my growth toward independence is being limited—we're growing apart.

The last semester in seminary, while writing my thesis, I move into the attic of a professor to write. I find I like the solitude. By now, I'm part of a strong support group of lesbian MCC clergy and am ready to candidate for pastor of an MCC church, maybe the one in Baltimore, my old coming-out feminist home. In Fall of 1981, after seven supportive and transforming years together, I leave Sibbie, who soon partners with another woman in the church. I move into the attic of a church member, then to a studio apartment off Dupont Circle with Zar, a white Siamese. I'm ready to move on.

While I'm finding myself as a newly single lesbian and a newly licensed minister living on a minimal salary, I visit a scared young man in the hospital who is dying of a newly identified disease called Acquired Immune Deficiency Syndrome. The rainbow weft of my life and the life of the LGBTQ community darkens.

5
New Weave

The TV lights glare bright in my eyes, makeup cakes my face, the director calls "3, 2, 1 . . . live," and the red light of the camera blinks on. I am the new lesbian pastor in Baltimore—newsworthy in 1982—on set for my first TV interview. Oprah Winfrey and Richard Sheer, cohosts of this morning call-in talk show, sit next to me, mics clipped to our clothes. Earnest in my clerical collar and gray pantsuit, palms slick with sweat, breath quick, I describe our church for gays and lesbians, an ecumenical Christian community that preaches God's love for all people. Sheer asks, "Have you just not met the right man yet?" a sneer on his pasty white face. I stammer a curt response, my guts twist.

One of the first callers is a fundamentalist Christian who quotes the Bible and uses words like "abomination." With tight hands and voice, I begin to spew verses of scripture, when Oprah leans toward me, whispers, "Invite him to your church." I breathe out, grateful for her support, face the red light of the camera, and welcome the man to worship with us, to see for himself the love I know is there.

I'm proud to stand for my people—but what if he really comes on Sunday? I call the Board to let them know about the invitation and on Sunday preach about welcoming. We are safe here, we hold each other, we stand and sing our love; he doesn't show.

~

I soon discover that Metropolitan Community Church of Baltimore is a more colorful weave than MCC in Washington, DC. The Baltimore church is equally women and men, includes transgender people, and is about a third African American. Rev. Delores Berry, a dynamic Black lesbian preacher, has served the congregation in the past, the last pastor was a "high church" white gay man from Australia, and two of the deacons are Black lesbians. The congregation of about a hundred is primarily working class, with strong community roots, reflecting the diversity of the closeted LGBTQ population of the city.

The church has a long history of struggle since its founding in the early 1970s. Kicked out of the funeral home it worshipped in early on—folks arrived one Sunday morning to find the doors padlocked—then worshipping in a gay bar downtown. The more recent worship space was destroyed by a fire at St. John's Methodist church. Now, in 1982, we worship in a predominately Black Methodist church with a closeted gay pastor, in a gentrifying urban neighborhood. My first year as pastor, after two host church matrons observe me performing a Holy Union for a couple in the sanctuary, their congregation votes to prohibit Holy Unions in their church. In response, as they hoped, we move on, back to the fire-ravaged church. We worship in the former social hall with high windows, bare stone walls hung with red and gold fabric and a rainbow banner. My small, chilly office in the back is where I counsel folks and type the bulletin. We socialize downstairs in a dank room with low ceilings. Yet we receive a steady, warm reception from the host pastor and congregation. We thrive in this safe space and host varied alternatives to the bar scene: a fund-raising hot dog stand at Baltimore Orioles baseball games, picnics and spaghetti dinners, a softball team, lobbying City Council for a gay rights ordinance. As AIDS surfaces in Baltimore, an entire ward at Johns Hopkins Hospital houses gay men attended by doctors scrambling to fight an unknown disease. As a white, feminist lesbian, I launch into this diverse weave with my usual enthusiasm—and I have much to learn.

~

The Baltimore Gay Community Center decides to hold a Gay Pride parade along one of the main streets downtown, expanding from the annual celebration in a local park. The parade is a new step in openness. There will be more media coverage, and people lining the streets can more easily identify folks, which puts us at risk for discrimination at work and with family.

I decide we will create a banner for our church to carry in the parade and call a working session. About a dozen of

Pastor of MCC Baltimore in 1987.
Photo © 2021 JEB (Joan E. Biren).

us gather one afternoon to cut out a rainbow of felt arches in purple, blue, green, yellow, orange, and red, glue them to the black canvas, and insert a long wooden dowel. Beneath this rainbow logos, the words "MCC—One in the Spirit," also in rainbow colors, proclaim our message, the refrain of one of our favorite hymns.

The next day, when I arrive downtown for the parade, the new banner tucked under one arm and wearing my clerical collar, I find no one from the congregation there to march with me. Drag queens gather in full glory, the Community Center collects around its banner, but where are Chuck, Shelley, Dottie, Don, Hortense, and all? After a long wait and embarrassed search, determined to march, I persuade a young Jewish woman to carry the other end of the banner. Together we march in the parade, along streets lined with onlookers. As I walk, I note a few congregation members in the back of the crowd lining the sidewalk, observing at a safe distance. The next Sunday, no one says a word about their absence. I learn how fear rules in this community. I hang the banner behind the wooden altar in the

MCC Baltimore with its banner at the March on Washington for Gay Pride, October 1987.

church, where it remains for years, occasionally removed for use in later, more well-attended marches.

~

I enter the sterile, white room, see the dark bruises covering Michael's arms, vivid purple, black, sienna blotches of rough skin. I ask, "Is it painful?" He nods yes. Grueling chemotherapy briefly halts growth of the Kaposi's sarcoma, but as his hair begins to grow again, Michael sighs, "It all grows back soon enough."

Michael tells me he grew up in nearby Harrisburg, Pennsylvania, and moved to New York City after he came out, estranged from his mother. I plan to visit the City one weekend and ask Michael if he has any messages. He gives me the name of a woman friend, tells me where to find her, and asks me to give her his contact info. I find the woman at a table eating pizza with friends in a crowded bar one Saturday evening, disco music blaring. Unable to talk privately, I move up behind her, put my hand on her shoulder, give her Michael's address. She quietly thanks me and later joins with friends to send him a note. He keeps it at his bedside.

During one of my regular visits, Michael shares that he founded New York's Integrity USA chapter—support for gays in the Episcopal Church. He misses worship. After long negotiations, the doctor grants him a pass to leave the hospital to attend our service one Sunday. He sits in a long-sleeved shirt in a rear pew near the door; soft light from the tall gold and green tinted windows warms his back, joyful music his heart. During communion people come forward singly, as couples, in small groups. I tear off a piece from the homemade loaf, place it in their cupped hands, they dip it in the cup of tart red wine. I hold people and pray with them. For some it's the only hug they get all week, for others it's public affirmation of their relationship, for newcomers it can be the first time they've received communion since childhood—they cry.

Michael doesn't come forward. At the end I walk back to his pew, give him the bread and wine, pray, hold him. Tears swallow his cheeks, he shakes, and I tremble—we share the pain of full life lost.

Soon enough, the IV needle won't insert in his arm as the splotches spread. He transfers down a floor to the silent, antiseptic, terminal ward, where lights are dim, treatment suspended. His mother drives down from Harrisburg. Michael's purple arms hold his mother's hands tenderly, gently, in pain and forgiveness. "We're having a love fest," he tells me. Hearts heal as disease devours the body's holding.

In the predawn a friend calls—"Michael just died." I drive downtown in the dark, through deserted streets, pass the nurses barricaded behind the circular counter, hurry down the silent hall, enter the room with Michael's still form, shades drawn, his mother leaning on the bed rail at his side, head bowed. I lean forward next to her, elbow resting on the bed rail, arm around her bent shoulder. We mourn in silence.

The funeral is up in Harrisburg. His mom, a few of her friends, Michael's friend Eddie, and I are the only attendees. Eddie chokes up when he reads Michael's letter to everyone—"I love you all." No one from New York attends.

6
Torn Weave

When Mother dies in 1978, our family tears apart, as does St. James in Knoxville, where Father pastors. Mother was an important partner in his ministry, and the church grieves her absence. When I visit the church, I'm startled to see Jennie Boyd Bull—her name and mine—engraved on the marble steps leading up to the altar, chiseled there in memoriam by parishioners, at eye level as they kneel for communion. On the outside wall, a pink marble plaque marks where her ashes are interred, across the courtyard garden from the statue of her beloved St. Francis.

My traditionalist father is incompetent at providing for himself at home, although John, Susan, Thanh, and I team up to buy him a microwave for Christmas, to help with the cooking. Grandmother Bull, his long-widowed mother and a pastor's wife, moves in from Charleston, South Carolina. He mortgages the house to build a separate room and bath for her, an expense he cannot afford. Grandmother tries to fill Mother's role in the church—after only a year, the women elect her head of the Episcopal Church Women. She initiates a needlework project for cushions at the altar rail—a petite steel magnolia.

~

In 1982, after Zar the cat and I have settled into an apartment in Charles Village in Baltimore, just two blocks away from where I first lived communally a decade earlier, I begin to look for a partner in MCC. I find Linda, a dark-haired librarian with an artistic flair, innate generosity, big brown eyes, and a warm sense of humor. She's a cat lover like me and plays energetic floor hockey with friends on the weekends. Linda's previous relationships have all been with Black lesbians, including an opera singer. I'm her first white love.

Linda works at Baltimore County Public Library, where she oversees the $3 million acquisitions budget for the large 15-branch library system, known for its stance of "give 'em what they want." She comes from a close Baltimore family—her father a librarian before her—and attended a private school near her family home in Pikesville. We often visit the family vacation home on Lake Nuangola in the Poconos of Western Pennsylvania.

One winter evening in Linda's apartment, as we stand next to the dining room table, I tell her I've discovered we share the same birthday—April 23—two years apart. Linda shoves me in the stomach and sinks to the floor, where she sits unspeaking. Stunned and scared, I back away. What just happened? The next day she admits fear that my birthday will overshadow hers. I'm beginning to understand the power differences as a pastor with my new partner, tread cautiously. In April, we hold a joint birthday party at her apartment, which helps her to move past the distrust.

When I show up one Sunday morning at church with a passion mark on my neck, visible even in my high-collared white robe, women in the congregation tease me as we socialize after service. This new interweaving of our lives is so public. To avoid the spectacle, we choose to hold a small, private rite of blessing of our relationship in Linda's home.

~

With the support of the Baltimore congregation, I chair MCC's denominational Faith, Fellowship, and Order Commission, charged with developing a theology and curriculum integrating spirituality and sexuality. What is spirituality? What is sexuality? Our FFO international team develops a series of queries and a workshop to help our people affirm their sexuality and explore how it interweaves with spirituality in their lives.

At the FFO workshop, I hand out paper and pen, ask folks to create an impromptu graph timeline of their sexual life, coming out, and relationships, then a separate graph of their spiritual life and transformations. Next, I ask them to place one timeline on top of the other and hold them both up to the light. What do they notice? I hear gasps and "O my God, loving my gay self matches loving God!" as they discover intersections, overlaps, opening to greater integration and wholeness. I find the work creative and satisfying, and so further hone my skills at creating international networks and educational structures for diverse people. How to bring these discoveries home to weave into my own life?

~

After a few months of blissful dating, Linda and I merge households; her tabby Pipher joins my Zar, and we soon adopt shy Scooter. We move into a typical Baltimore row house near the church—narrow, two-story brick, with marble steps along the sidewalk and a tiny back yard with chain-link fence next to the alley. We fill the house with multiple tall shelves of Linda's books, hang a quilt top on the wall, pieced by Grandmother Boyd using fabric from her husband's shirts and daughter's dresses. I frame and hang two of Linda's watercolors over the mantel.

In a couple of years, Linda and I have saved enough to buy our own home in Lauraville, an old, interracial neighborhood next to a city park and Morgan State University, with big frame houses and ample yards. Old sycamore trees shade the streets. I marvel there is so much light in this house—windows on four sides, spacious rooms, a fireplace for winter nights, a sunroom where I meditate, a dining room with a wall of built-in cabinets. We drink tea in the evenings on the patio under the tall oak in the back yard. I grow a small garden out back along the fence across from the garage. Linda installs a potter's wheel in the basement, next to the many shelves of books. We are happy here.

I slowly connect with the Baltimore lesbian feminist community—at first they are suspicious of this Christian pastor. I join Linda's women's book group—we vacation with them at Rehoboth Beach—and find a weekly lesbian support group, where I make friends who are chosen family to this day. Linda and these women offer acceptance, support, and deep listening through difficult days to come.

~

Only two years after Mother's death, after dating three women in the church at the same time, Father chooses to marry Ruth, a divorced mother of four with two teenage girls at home. I've heard the story that all three of the women he has been dating show up one Easter Sunday wearing identical corsages he gave them—what was he thinking? Brother John and I come for the wedding and stand as witnesses beside Ruth's daughters. As a wedding present, I embroider matching pillowcases with their initials. Mother died when I was only 33, and Father remarries 3 years later. I'm trying hard to be open to this new relationship.

When he marries Ruth, the congregation erupts in discord led by one of the rejected women. Eventually the bishop transfers him to another congregation—a sad ending after thirty years of service. The discord spills over at home, where Ruth and Grandmother vie for dominance. Within a year Grandmother has moved back to South Carolina.

~

At home, Linda and I reach some hard places around money. We begin couples therapy, seek out a lesbian therapist in nearby DC because we are too well known in Baltimore. My pastor's salary is minimal—finances are always a tension in our lives. Although I always pay my fair share of the mortgage and bills, it is Linda who buys the extra food, the new clothes, theater tickets, vacations, meals out at our favorite Thai restaurant. Linda's innate generosity is a blessing in our lives, yet sometimes my self-esteem suffers in the contrast.

I continue in individual therapy for several years, integrating grief over Mother's death and reclaiming her presence in me, along with grief over the stench of death that hangs over the gay community and in my gut as so many die of AIDS. Through these hard times, opening to more fully know myself, I begin bodywork to release the stress, study Tai Chi to integrate body and mind.

At the same time, Linda is going through her own transformation, accepting that she is an overeater, addicted to secretive daily quarts of Häagen-Dazs almond mocha ice cream. She now regularly attends Overeaters Anonymous meetings, uses a measuring cup to portion everything she eats, and finds a new community of OA friends. We're both working hard on ourselves.

We adopt our black Lab, Daisy Mae, an exuberant puppy who brings joy to our lives. Her full name is Daisy Mae Romeo Thompson Boyd Bull W. For years, Daisy is my companion on long walks in the woods and mountains surrounding Baltimore. Her nose always finds the way home.

~

After Grandmother's exit, Ruth, John, and teen daughters have the house to themselves, and Ruth begins to alienate and exclude the rest of the family. First, Father announces that he has rewritten his will, leaving everything, which is not much—the house in town and a tiny log cabin in the mountains—to Ruth and her daughters. When I visit Knoxville, Father and I sit at the dining room table and discuss the will. I tell him my future is secure with Linda, so I'm not concerned for my financial needs, but he and John built that log cabin together long before Mother died, and he and Ruth never visit it. The land and cabin should go to my brother. I'm satisfied to hear later that he revised the will to give the mountain property to John.

~

I begin a deeper spiritual struggle with my faith, with the maleness of Jesus. How can I know the embodiment of Christ within me if he is man and I am a woman? How can I surrender to the authority of a man spiritually? I've moved beyond God the Father and know the indwelling of the Holy Spirit, but who is God the Son to me?

I preach sermons, write articles, agonize in therapy and support groups, and gradually find that I have moved to the fringes of MCC, increasingly viewed by some in the congregation as a radical feminist who doesn't preach the "Gospel." For centuries, the church has used the maleness of Jesus to justify excluding women—I'm not alone on this one. The embodied struggle is deeply personal and painful. I strive to hold these wrestlings close—I'm such a public figure in the community that anonymity is not an option.

~

I've been pastor of MCC Baltimore for six years now, confident in the leadership I'm cultivating to build our community. Bob and Richard are competent student clergy and treasurer respectively, Hortense a caring deacon as she tends her paralyzed son, shot after his release from prison. Cynthia gives administrative support three days a week. Deacon Don brings leadership on the district board, even though he also still attends his conservative Black Baptist church on Sunday mornings. I especially benefit from Shelley's hours of copying and collation for FFO and the Board's support of times away at MCC conferences and National Council of Churches meetings. Chuck and Bob, Terry and Jude visit their City Council members to lobby for a gay rights ordinance—they've come a long way out of the closet.

The MCC caucus of women clergy supports my personal therapy; I feel safe, nurtured, and strong as we move forward together toward a more inclusive community. In sermons, I explore the Hebraic wisdom of Sophia and John's gospel of "the Word made flesh," incarnation as embodiment. The new AIDS interfaith network I've helped to launch offers support in AIDS ministry. I enjoy counseling couples for Holy Unions, using family systems training from seminary. The work is challenging, but I'm tough, feel supported and up for it.

Then it all tears apart.

Adam, district coordinator, calls a meeting in our church basement with board, staff, and me to inform us that much of the church leadership—Bob and Richard, Hortense, Don, and others—is forming a new church, led by Frank, the retired Methodist clergy who rarely attends. I'm devastated—this is the first I've heard of this desertion. Adam asks why he heard about it in Los Angeles at MCC headquarters before I hear about it here? They look down and don't respond. Who are they working with? It seems Don gathered support from my old MCC in Washington, DC, whose pastor Larry—my former mentor, soon to die of AIDS—has called our congregation "a spiritual wasteland."

The warp of my heart threatens to snap—I didn't see this backlash coming. I feel betrayed, undercut, devalued, exposed. It's especially hard to see leaders in the church break away, people I trusted and worked with daily. I whine to friends, "They think they know enough now to do it on their own." I soldier on—the new group dies out in less than a year—but the damage to my heart remains. This is not a safe space.

~

One holiday, Linda and I sit at the dining room table to plan our drive down to Knoxville to see Father and Ruth. I open the mail to read a letter from Father: "You are welcome to come, but Linda is not. We have young girls in the house." I bang the paper down on the table, close my eyes to darkness, hug my denim jacket, smell rage, breath ragged, deep. When I tell Linda, she says she never liked him anyway, withdraws. We don't go.

After all these years of support, why has he sided with Ruth's bigotry? Who is this weak man to me now? Not the father

I've pedestaled all my life, the wise preacher in the pulpit. The sound of his fall is long and hard.

The rejection continues. In later years, when an aunt invites us to a Bull family gathering at the family home in Georgetown, South Carolina, Ruth objects to our lesbian presence. It's a rough, alienating time—my brother John and sister Susan have their own versions of rejection, with other rationales. Gradually, we each withdraw from his new family and lose contact even with each other, although we've reconnected again more recently.

~

The pain of bigotry cuts across all layers of my life. In 1981, I participate in MCC's application for membership in the National Council of Churches, attend several NCC meetings to present our application. The NCC is an ecumenical body of 34 Protestant and Eastern Orthodox churches in the U.S., known for its social activism; it does not include Roman Catholic or Evangelical Christians. In the 1980s, only a few denominations show any support for LGBTQ people—the Unitarians, some Quakers, the United Church of Christ. Our application is divisive; the Eastern Orthodox churches threaten to walk out if we are admitted.

Two Eastern Orthodox men slip into our MCC suite at the hotel and sit in the corner; the room goes silent. My friend Karen, brave pastor of MCC New York, walks over to them, sits down close, and says, "You are the people we are afraid of. Thank you for coming." In later years, Eastern Orthodox gays form their own support group.

Letty Russell, a closeted feminist theologian at Yale and an NCC activist, attends the meeting with her partner and other women friends. They quietly invite me to their room for drinks one evening. Letty is a bit condescending toward MCC, presents her biblical interpretations as authoritative. I look her in the eyes as I leave and say, "I hope our presence here has supported you in some way." I validate our outlier role in pressuring the hierarchy, where she has chosen to remain closeted for safety.

NCC tables the application for membership and votes for "further study," on the grounds that gay and lesbian identity is not a criterion for a denomination. The next church group admitted to the NCC is the Korean Presbyterian Church. As observers seated in the back of the hall, we stand in protest, a silent witness. Tears run down my cheeks. Is nationality a criterion for a denomination?

MCC appoints me to the NCC Faith and Order Commission, where I attend meetings to present our theological and biblical stance. About 20 clergy from different denominations, including four of us from MCC, sit around a large conference table and answer questions about scripture, its historical interpretation condemning homosexuality, and MCC's interpretation that these passages do not apply to loving, committed same-gender relationships. One theologian asks me, "So, is this a new revelation?" I catch that he is trying to trap us into stating we are outside orthodox faith, so respond, "No, this is not a new revelation about scripture; we are asking new questions. We teach a liberation theology, an oppressed people seeking truth in scripture that speaks to our condition."

I address the NCC assembly, tell them, "Ministering in the gay and lesbian community is hard; we ask for your prayers."

~

Father and Ruth are married for over twenty years and seem to love each other. He has someone to take care of him in his old age, and she has financial security for the rest of her life. After he retires, they can't afford to keep the mortgaged house, so buy a small condo across town and live simply. He still smokes, even after surviving quintuple bypass heart surgery, which adds another decade to his life, with mild mental decline. Ruth and her daughters care for him. My occasional visits are awkward, brief. He laments not having grandchildren, that I have "abandoned my Christian faith."

~

By 1991, the World Council of Churches, with 349 denominations in more than 110 countries, grants observer status to MCC, which continues to participate actively in its meetings. But never the U.S. National Council. MCC continues to attend NCC meetings for eleven more long years, from 1981 to 1992, when NCC denies its application for observer status. As Dennis Hevesi writes in *The New York Times*:

> In a 90-to-81 vote on Thursday at its annual convention in Cleveland . . . the National Council of Churches chose not to grant observer status to . . . the Universal Fellowship of

Metropolitan Churches, a denomination that has 50,000 members in 264 congregations around the country.

Primary opponents to granting observer status had been the Eastern Orthodox churches, some of the African-American denominations and the Korean Presbyterian Church in the United States. There were 12 denominations which . . . said that if observer status were granted they would be forced to leave the council.

The announcement touched off an emotional demonstration by members of the church at the hotel where the meeting was held, as well as by gay and lesbian representatives from denominations that already belong to the council. The [MCC] ecumenical officer, . . . the Rev. Nancy Wilson, stepped to the microphone in the meeting room and said, "It's easier to get into heaven than into the N.C.C."

~

Father dies of recurrent non-Hodgkins lymphoma in 2002 at age 84, in a nursing home the last few months, depressed and distant. When I visit him the last time, a few weeks before his death, he seems to recognize me but is not responsive. I try to feed him by spoon and he mutters, "Everyone stops by on their way to somewhere else."

When I come back to Knoxville for the funeral, as I walk in the front door to a room filled with relatives, Ruth hands me a manila envelope with some family photos and announces, "Here's is what you're getting and that's all." John and Susan receive the same. Susan sobs, "At least she could have given me a pair of Father John's cuff links or something."

At the funeral, the retired bishop who preaches has mild dementia and can't remember much about Father's life. Yes, he served on the mission board that created several new congregations around Knoxville, but that's not all. I resent the omissions. The combined family dinner after, with Ruth's daughters—the first time we've all sat down together—is awkward, filled with silences. We never hear from Ruth again.

~

In turmoil, I resign as pastor of MCC Baltimore in May 1989. That summer, I settle into a new job as manager of the 31st Street Bookstore, a women's and children's bookstore in Baltimore and a cultural center for the feminist community, grateful for the support of Linda and women friends.

Death, whether of body or connection, is a profound teacher, some say the best teacher. I've spent the last seven years immersed in pastoring in the LGBTQ community in Baltimore, which means I've held the hands and hearts of dying gay men, their lovers, and families. I've survived the re-weave of family and estrangement with Father's remarriage, the tearing apart of the church I pastor, and the exclusion in the turmoil of the wider Christian church. Now it's time to let go.

I'm like my mother in many ways. I weave her nurturing spirit and hard work "against the odds" with Father's intellectual curiosity. I've learned from her the courage to persist through difficulties, yet the pain of institutional and family homophobia tears my heart; death and exclusion force me deeper into an inner journey of loving myself. I can't get it together to stand up and preach every Sunday and still fall apart in exploring all the textures within me, so I make one of the toughest and best decisions of my life—I choose to take the time away from supporting others to support my own growth, to mend the torn weave.

7
Radiant Weft

Sitting in my wooden chair, I gaze out the window into the back yard with the big oak tree and close my eyes to meditate. In this stillness of mind, spasms of energy move my body—shoulders twitch, neck jerks, and spine writhes. The power of this fiery energy scares me, so I reach out to a friend, who lends me a book by an Indian Guru who describes *kriyas*, purifying movements of the *shakti*, spiritual energy. Tucked into the book is a small photograph of a young Indian woman, a meditation master, who gazes at me with intense brown eyes filled with love. The love in her eyes draws me in, so I begin to hold her photo as I meditate. I now trust that the power of this fiery energy will transform my life, confirmed later when I learn that the gaze of a meditation master has the power to give *shaktipat*, awakening the *kundalini shakti*, the spiritual energy within a seeker. Her eyes awaken me to that experience.

The *kundalini shakti* clears the energetic pathways, moves upward from the base of the spine along the spinal column to the crown of the head, to merge with this same *shakti* everywhere. Today's science confirms this ancient mystical truth in the discovery that vibrating energy sustains all life, from electromagnetic waves to neurons. I yearn to relax into the inner silence, experience the pulsation of the *shakti*, recognize and honor that same love and life in all.

As I meditate a few weeks later, I clutch the photo as I struggle to trust my body, its memories, the painful truths it holds, the questions of neglect and trauma that choke my throat. Jesus and the Indian woman come to me in meditation. Jesus stands on the left and the woman on the right. They each place a hand on my chest and envelop me with waves of healing love, their warmth radiating from my heart throughout my body. I burst into tears and know they both love me, are part of me, and there is no conflict between them—I am loved and loveable. Their love weaves a radiant new thread of light and hope into my life. I name this experience "the handover."

~

As the new manager of the feminist 31st Street Bookstore collective in my old Waverly neighborhood, I enjoy the company of the many women and children who come by the store, learn the ropes of ordering books from feminist and mainstream presses, and rely on the board and many volunteers who make it all happen. The store carries most of the titles from small, feminist presses: Cleis, Firebrand, Kitchen Table, Naiad, Seal, New Victoria, Spinster/Aunt Lute. Our collections emphasize fiction and poetry, stocking a third feminist publications, a third lesbian, and a third "international women of color." Nonfiction titles deal with violence against women, spirituality, ecofeminism, vegetarian cooking, and women's biography. *The Courage to Heal* (incest recovery) and *Creation Fire* (Caribbean women's poetry) are bestsellers. The children's room in the back specializes in multicultural and special interest paperbacks—*Heather Has Two*

31st Street Bookstore Cooperative at March on Washington in 1993.

Mommies, *The People Could Fly*, and a lesbian parenting section. Cards, calendars, CDs of women's music from Ladyslipper, and other sidelines make up a quarter of the bookstore's sales. Our bookstore is the retail arm and cultural center of the feminist movement in Baltimore.

One morning, as I sit for meditation in the stillness of dawn, the phone rings. I hurry to answer—don't want to wake Linda. The bookstore has been broken into. I grab on clothes, run to the car, and drive down empty, dark streets to the bookstore. Jagged corners of shattered glass glitter in the streetlight. A gaping hole reveals the register and counter, card racks and shelves exposed. "What's inside? What's outside?" No boundaries, only invasive violence, exposing the entrails of the store I manage.

I call board members, give police the info they need, begin to shake. My hands tremble as I peer inside, to find the register cracked open—no money gone, no further theft. Then I see the dirty red brick on the floor covered in shards of plate glass. "Was this a drive-by vandal?" The bookstore has been here in Waverly for over twenty years. "Why would anyone invade us? Why are they mad at us? as lesbians? leftists? or just another store with money?"

I sit down at my desk in the back corner, think to call Dan, the landlord, about replacing the window, call Linda, find someone to guard the store while I go home for breakfast and a much-needed hug. I'm grateful for the collective—others will help.

~

A few weeks after the handover experience in meditation, when I'm working at the front desk of the bookstore, one of the board members drops by and lets me know about a group that gathers each week to chant and meditate. I've been missing the singing at church and decide to visit the group for its weekly *satsang* of chanting and meditation.

The evening of October 30, 1989, I walk up the steps to a home in Mount Washington, luminaria lighting the walkway, and enter a darkened attic room blazing with candlelight and the sweet fragrance of incense. I am ecstatic to recognize that the photo of the woman in the chair at the front of the room is the same as the woman in the photo I've been holding in meditation. I find the source of this new heart-opening love in her eyes. We sit quietly on the floor, on cushions, and then begin to sing an Indian chant, *"Hare Rama, Hare Krishna,"* men and women alternating lines. I've never chanted before, much less sat for an hour on the floor with my back unsupported. I manage to remain upright by tensing my back and stomach muscles for the chant and meditation following. I don't know anyone and feel a bit awkward in this small, obviously heterosexual, mostly white, educated group, but resolve to return. At some deep level I know I'm home.

When I return for *satsang* the next week, there are no lights along the walk, but the lights and meditation and chanting remain inside the hall where we gather. I learn that my first visit was on the Indian festival of lights, *Diwali,* which marks the Indian new year, an auspicious inaugural day. I begin to attend regularly and to offer s*eva*, volunteer service, with their bookstore, read the autobiography of her Guru, and purchase a photo of the Teacher and incense for my meditation space at home. I know I'm entering a whole new culture of images and vocabulary and metaphors, which is daunting at first, but I deeply trust the heart-opening love from the Teacher. Every time I look at her eyes in the photo, my heart races and chills run up my spine and out the top of my head. I listen to my body and heart and keep showing up. Linda initially resists, jealous of my focus on the Teacher; she holds internal arguments with her during meditation. But eventually Linda, too, experiences that loving presence and begins to attend *satsangs*. I also start saving for the day-long meditation event the following Spring when I will receive spiritual awakening from the Teacher. Can there be even more such love?

On Easter, April 15, 1990, I participate in a meditation intensive transmitted by satellite from the ashram in India where the Teacher resides. I'm wearing my favorite blue and pink handwoven top that Linda gave me, and two pendants—the risen Christ with arms outstretched and the Goddess with arms upraised. This is the first time I have seen the Teacher on live camera, moving and speaking and smiling and singing. Her words speak directly to my heart's questions because she teaches that God dwells within everything and everyone, including each of us.

Joined by thousands around the world, my heart and voice respond to hers as we sing the final chant. I feel the river of love flow back and forth between us, in and out with each breath. Suddenly, the Christ and Goddess pendants merge into a dancing, many-armed divine figure in my heart—we are One. I soon learn this is Shiva Nataraj, the primordial Teacher who has emerged in my heart. Shiva is the dancing deity who creates, sustains, destroys, conceals, and reveals the highest truth. The divine silence of Shiva and pulsation of Shakti, male and female, merge into one radiant Truth.

I am ecstatic—laughing, crying, shaking with love. As I sit in the back of the hall while others gather to leave, I deeply know that the Guru is always with me because she now lives in my heart. I resolve that faith in that internal love will sustain me to grow in her grace. I take this teaching to live by, and to this day remember it when I doubt the spiritual power and love that are within me. Since it is easy for me to focus on the external, the physical form of things, I've always been grateful for this first teaching that the true divine presence is within.

After everyone has left, I'm still too ecstatic to drive, so I lie down on the green grass and look up at the trees and birds and sky and laugh and laugh and laugh and laugh. Everything is greener, bluer, brighter. My eyes are open to a new way of seeing.

~

The following week, Linda and I leave for a two-week trip to Europe to visit her sister in Paris and travel around England and Scotland. The trip becomes a pilgrimage to my roots in Western religious culture, a journey of gratitude, of letting go and moving on. At Chartres, I walk the labyrinth, lay a stone from the Eastern mountains in the center, and then visit the shrine to the Mother Goddess in the crypt on which the cathedral was built. In England, near Hadrian's Wall, we take a taxi to visit Long Meg and Her Daughters, a prehistoric circle of stones surrounding a monolithic *menhir*, settled beside a country farmhouse. I offer a stone and receive one in return, a small goddess figure. All this time, I am ecstatic and focused, filled with wonder and devotion and gratitude.

When we reach the Scottish seaside village of Oban and take the train over to Edinburgh, my body reaches its physical limits and I get sick. By the next day, when we travel back down to tiny Coleshill outside Birmingham, the home of my

Bull family ancestors, I'm at my emotional limit. We walk into the 14th century Coleshill parish church, with a plaque to one of my Bull ancestors and an even more ancient Norman baptismal font, present since 1086. When a young woman in clerical collar walks down the aisle to greet us, I burst into hysterical sobs. The Church of England has just begun to ordain women, and my heart sees in this young woman the end of centuries of women's exclusion and hope for the future. I can't begin to express all of this and run outside to lean against a wall, squat in the dirt and cry. I know that in past lives I lived in this place and was denied what this woman is now living. Some deep healing is taking place in my body, both for me and for the Church.

We conclude our visit at Westminster Abbey, where we attend evensong, seated in the choir up front near the altar, its dark wooden pews carved with gargoyles, alongside tombs of bishops. Organ music soars to the marble vault, and our voices rise in beloved ancient psalms of praise. There I offer gratitude for all I have received from my ancestors, as I move into a future spirituality that crosses races, classes, cultures, and histories, into an expanded, future interweaving of multicolored weft and warp and breath and life.

~

One of the first things I learn from the Teacher is to love her Guru. I dream he welcomes me to an Indian courtyard, where he is seated at a feast with followers. He gestures to me, "Come, join the feast." I accept—allow myself to be nourished at his table. When I visit India later, I understand the dream was in the courtyard of his ashram in India. And because I've learned to love him, within the next year I find myself driving back to Knoxville to reconcile with Father, chanting the Guru's name the whole way. The visit is awkward, but I gather the courage to tell Father I forgive him for excluding Linda, insist that we take a walk outside when he lights up a cigarette. We remain distantly connected until his death.

~

As I attend the meditation center *satsangs*, I pitch in on workdays to support the expanding community as we create a new meditation space. We rent and renovate an old restaurant on the ground floor of an apartment building in Charles Village a few blocks from Waverly. We scrub the kitchen grease off the walls, repaint everything, and build a beautiful new home for worship: deep red carpet in the meditation hall, sweet incense in the air, and flowers by the Guru's chair, a welcome desk at the entrance, café with kitchenette, and bookstore with glass windows. At first, I coordinate the bookstore, using skills from 31st Street Bookstore. Then I begin to serve on the committee that plans weekly *satsangs* and other events. My experience in coordinating volunteers and in public speaking is an asset. I listen and learn and meditate and chant.

Over the next few years, I become part of the center steering committee, then serve on the regional steering committee, helping to create systems and structures for this growing path. I stand in *satsang* to share my meditation experiences. I visit the ashram on the East Coast, where the Teacher resides when she is not on tour or at her ashram in India. I drive the several hours north to the ashram for vacations and long weekends, volunteer there as a cashier in the snack bar, walk the paths in the woods, and chant ecstatically with the Teacher in the evenings. I'm finding a new way to serve, as the weft shifts its radiant colors.

~

Managing the 31st Street Bookstore is both a delight and a challenge. In 1992, we create a bulletin board display of T-shirts with political slogans from the rich progressive and feminist history of Baltimore in the 1970s and '80s—"Womon Power," "Sisters Unite," "The Hand that Rocks the Cradle," "Ain't I a Woman," "Uppity Girls." We sponsor Adrienne Rich, Kay Gardner, and Sonia Johnson for readings and workshops. Our book table at Campfest, the local women's music festival, is a money-maker. In 1991, *Publishers Weekly* runs a feature article on the success of the collective's efforts. The mayor appoints me to the new Baltimore City Commission for Women. In 1992, I receive the Community Service Award from the Passages Conference run by Washington and Baltimore lesbians, nominated by bookstore board members and friends.

We also have our struggles, as do many small, independent bookstores. Borders and Barnes & Noble, the big chain bookstores, come to town in 1993. One infamous afternoon, a woman visits the store, walks to the back room, and takes notes on our feminist periodical inventory. As she leaves, she announces, "I'm a book buyer for Borders." I am livid. For a city that has never offered anything but small, private or college bookstores, the lure of the big box stores in the upscale suburb of Towson is too strong. Our sales tank.

In 1994, our bookstore closes its doors after 25 years. It's a hard time for me as manager. My weekly women's group offers much-needed support. I tell them, "How would you like to be manager when the bookstore goes out of business?" I call Lammas, the women's bookstore in DC, and ask the owner, "Would you like to buy a bookstore?" To my surprise, she says yes, purchases the inventory, and moves the new Baltimore branch of Lammas downtown to a few blocks away from Lambda Rising, the gay men's bookstore, and out of the historically progressive Waverly neighborhood. Predictably, the store folds in a couple of years, as do many feminist bookstores and presses in the 1990s, as women's liberation goes uptown. Read *The Disappearing L*, by Bonnie Morris, to learn more about this era of declining lesbian culture.

My bookstore years are a time of changing weft in my life, of overlapping colors and threads. The radiant new Indian weft now sustains me.

8
Fiery Weft

I'm almost 50 and out of a job again. Linda is most supportive, bless her heart. She lands me an interview with the large, 15-branch Baltimore County Public Library system where she works as head of Materials Selection. Together, she and I select a green-and-red-leaf patterned skirt for me to wear to the interview, a red knit top, and tights to cover my hairy legs. I'm nervous, but manage to answer the interviewer's question, "What would you say if someone asked you for a book about cats?" I reply, "That could mean anything—care and feeding, *The Cat in the Hat* by Dr. Seuss, Rita Mae Brown mysteries. I'd ask them for more information." I later learn the reference interview techniques of "Can you tell me more?" "Does that completely answer your question?" They hire me as a library associate. With a year of on-the-job training, I'm certified as a librarian and work at the Pikesville then Randallstown branches close to our home for the next seven years, 1994–2001.

~

For my fiftieth birthday in 1995, Linda gives me a surprise birthday party and a most generous gift. She has requested donations from family and friends, many of them not following our Indian path, so I can travel to the ashram in Maharashtra, India. At the party, I receive a check for $2,000, enough for airfare and the minimal costs of room and board. I'm overwhelmed with gratitude. The following winter, I fly to India. I've just begun the library job, and they give me a month off for the trip—amazing!

I live in the tropical world of the ashram in Maharashtra for a month, where I learn word processing and data entry upstairs in the computer offices above the temple, transcribing oral interviews about the history of the path. Although the Teacher is living in the ashram in the U.S. at the time, I feel close to her and her Guru as I revel in this sacred space he created and where she spent many of her weekends and school vacations growing up. The ashram is lush and green in contrast to the dusty road and fields outside. Fountains splash, coconut trees give fresh milk to drink, mango trees drop their luscious fruit, and a many-rooted banyan tree anchors the garden path. I absorb the fragrance of bougainvillea and frangipani, meditate in the marble courtyard of my dream, and eat vegetarian meals with my fingers, sitting in silence on grass mats. Each day, I rise before dawn to meditate and chant the morning chant, offer *seva*, then chant again before lunch, nap during the heat of midday. Then it's back to *seva*, evening worship in the Temple followed by a simple supper, final chant in the courtyard, and early to bed. My knowledge of the path and its origins deepens, as do my commitment and inner journey. The Indian weave radiates fragrant love and silence.

~

I flourish while working at the Pikesville and Randallstown libraries, which serve diverse communities. I learn much about Jewish and Black culture in the suburbs north of Baltimore and from the immigrants speaking 17 different languages who walk through the doors of the Randallstown branch each week. Libraries are the gateway to democracy for our patrons, providing access to computer literacy, to information, to learning for children and students, and much more. I coordinate the Helping Hands team, a service group of African American professionals at Verizon who volunteer each afternoon to staff the computer sign-up desk, new to libraries in the 1990s. They also offer regular computer classes, show grandmothers how to set up email accounts to stay in touch with their children, and assist students with online research. I learn to maintain and weed collections, answer challenging reference questions, and create children's programs. One year I chair the system's Newbery Committee, which reads and selects the best juvenile fiction published each year. I enjoy working with the multicultural staff at Randallstown and end up as a diversity trainer with the library system.

~

On our birthday in 1997, Linda and I drive to her mother's brick home north of Baltimore on the edge of Sudbrook Park, a tree-

Jennie as a librarian in 1994.

lined residential neighborhood of old Victorian houses designed by Frederick Law Olmsted. We are taking Linda's mother and visiting sister out to dinner to celebrate our birthdays. On arriving, a neighbor tells us her mother has just been taken to the hospital. She had complained of indigestion before her nap, and the sister later found her collapsed on the bedroom floor. We rush to the hospital to join the family and hold vigil in the tiny, sterile family lounge. A young doctor enters and in monotone informs us, "She is dead of a heart attack." Linda shrieks and embraces her sister while I stand helpless. We enter the treatment room to view her pale and invaded form—shunts in her groin and arms—then drive back to the house, dazed with the shock of sudden death.

We all grieve Linda's mom. She was kind and accepting of me because she knew Linda and I loved each other. On my first meal with the family years earlier, she pronounced, "You'll do, but you eat too fast." Linda and her older sister, both "unmarried," inherit the house, and we arrange to buy out her sister. The next Spring, we renovate the house to let in more light, expand the living room, and add a picture window. We sell our home in Lauraville and move into our new home in Pikesville, along with dogs Chelsea and Daisy Mae and cats Zar and Pipher.

While this is a good financial decision, I forget to consider that Linda grew up in this house and it has many memories for her, heightened by her grief. As Linda grieves in this house, she maintains her eating recovery but takes on some of her parents' demanding behaviors. I'm working hard on childhood issues in therapy. Our relationship begins to fray, physical intimacy ends, and we grow apart in the burden of unresolved grief.

~

My term on the regional steering committee of my meditation path has ended. It's time to take the next step, but what comes next? Could I move to the East Coast ashram to serve full time? I begin to save for another visit to the ashram in India, this time with my own funds. By 2000, I have saved enough money and visit the Maharashtra ashram again for a ten-day silent meditation retreat. I bring with me the tortured question of whether I should leave Linda and apply to live in the U.S. ashram, or whether we should continue our strained relationship.

Linda and I have been together for 18 years in a loving, joyful relationship. We have grown together in so many ways. Her family and work provide financial and emotional security. We own our home. I'm a respected member of the Baltimore lesbian community. I enjoy my work as a librarian, visit the East Coast ashram regularly, am a leader in the Baltimore meditation center. And I know that the Teacher is present in my heart. So why am I so drawn to give up years of community and security to move to the ashram? Part of the answer is yearning for deeper connection with the radiant *shakti* in my heart that I feel full-time service and life at the ashram will bring. Part is feeling stuck in an increasingly negative relationship and peering into a limited, deadening future of security chosen over growth. My heart is divided—how do I follow it?

The day of my return from India, we sit at the dining room table Father made, Linda across from me, not looking at me. She asks, "What did you decide?" I don't know for sure until I say the words. My heart is torn, the leap is far from what I know; the "good girl" disapproval weights my shoulders. I take a deep breath and say the words, make the choice. "I'm going to apply to live in the ashram." Linda grows even more pale, looks down, says nothing. The pain runs deep.

I move downstairs to the study to sleep, and remain there

until eight months later, a strained, awkward time. In the months that follow, Zar the cat dies of pneumonia. Both Chelsea and Daisy Mae reach the end and we put them down—I hold each of them as the vet injects the syringe. Linda's sister takes her on a month-long vacation in Germany, so she can get away. In May, the week I'm accepted on staff at the ashram, the Randallstown library where I work is badly damaged by fire. I've worked there for seven years, now vested for retirement income. The doors of my life in Baltimore close, one by one, in tortured synchronicity.

When I pack the car to leave in August, Linda's wail from the house screams in my ears as I back out of the driveway. When I arrive at the ashram, I discover that today, August 8, is a holiday, an auspicious day to begin my new life of service. I enthusiastically dive into the *seva* offered me and rejoice in the daily schedule of meditation and chanting, the delicious vegetarian meals, and worship in the Temple. In the Temple, I sometimes find myself in tears at the intensity of the change, both grieving and celebrating in the purifying presence of the Guru and my new life.

The broken threads tear away from the heartwood of the loom, leaving painful gaps and radiant new threads. Once again, I have chosen the fire of inner growth and transformation over commitment and security.

9
Whole Fabric

My fifteen years of service—from 2001 to 2015—at the East Coast ashram of my Indian spiritual path reweaves my life into a whole fabric. We are the hub for a meditation path serving followers all over the world, of all races and languages, with the majority living in India, the source of the teachings. The Guru, the spiritual head of the path, is both modern and timeless in her teaching. We live and serve to support her dissemination of the teachings around the world, using modern technology in livestream webcasts and an ever-changing website. I love the mix of tradition and innovation: classical Indian ragas with improvisation by a jazz pianist, ancient Indian rituals filmed and posted on the Internet, scriptures interpreted with funny contemporary stories. The Teacher loves and respects children. She encourages them to participate in our dancing circles and chants and creative projects.

    I live in a small room within one of the main ashram buildings, a former hotel room. I'm supported by the daily meditation, chanting, exercise, and nutritious vegetarian meals shared with ashram residents and the numerous followers who come for shorter visits as I used to do. It is true communal living, focused on the spiritual practices and service to support the work of the path. I rarely leave the ashram—maybe once a month for personal supplies—unless I venture out to kayak or hike in the nearby lakes and mountains. I volunteer to open the Temple for early morning worship, staff the library on Sunday afternoons, take hatha yoga and Tai Chi classes most mornings. It's a balanced life with a focus on service. I also make a few close women friends during my years there—a hiking buddy, a partner in Sanskrit study, and a creative puppeteer.

The challenge is in *seva*, the volunteer service with the global organization that absorbs most of my waking hours. We implement the Teacher's vision for disseminating the teachings as we create the global systems and structures necessary to support the path. I serve in several *sevas* and manage to gracefully transition from one to the other as requested over the years: executive assistant in the teachings area, editorial coordinator for the home study course, archivist for the Teacher's talks, head of the intellectual property department. All of them employ skills I've learned in previous work and open me to learn new skills, especially teamwork with the culturally diverse staff and volunteers.

I also seek to gain deeper knowledge of classical Indian scriptures. A friend and I take a class in Sanskrit at a nearby community college, then study from a Sanskrit language textbook, guided on weekly calls with a Sanskrit graduate student on the West Coast. Over the next couple of years—two verses a week on my days off—I translate into English the 182 verses of Shri Guru Gita, the ancient Sanskrit chant we recite each morning. I offer the translation to the Teacher, in gratitude for the ways that deeper study of this sacred scripture has transformed my understanding of its powerful Truth: "By the gift of the Guru's grace, one should contemplate the delight of the Self; by this path of the Guru, knowledge of one's own Self arises" (*Sri Guru Gita*, v. 110, my translation).

~

The solitude and beauty of the forests and mountains just minutes from my room draw me into their silence on my days off. I often ramble along the paths through the ashram's woods, and after a while I volunteer to maintain them. This gifts me with hours of delightful solitude. I watch beaver at their pond, deer crunching apples along the path, bluebirds flitting around the lake, and fox kits gamboling under the porch. Even the bear who meets me on a trail deep in the woods, surprised by my "tail" of a rake.

As I head out for the afternoon, I gather work gloves, rake, and nippers from the musty tool shed by the archive building with the wooden door that won't shut because pine needles clump in the jamb. The woods around the ashram are wild and thickly forested—fragrant pine, balsam, maple, oak, interspersed with two old beaver ponds, dead trunks rising from the water, the occasional heron. These woods protect the buildings and lawns and offer me space for quiet walks on Mondays off as I maintain the trails with rake in hand, nippers stuffed in the back pocket of my jeans. I snip branches that grow too close to the narrow paths, pull up or cut back weeds growing in the loam, rake leaves to the side, lift and toss branches fallen across the way. Sometimes I remove larger limbs with a small handsaw. Shadows dance, as delicate patterns of sunlight filter through the leaves. Fallen nurse logs grow moss and lichen and new trees. Felled trees with gnawed teeth marks signal the beaver pond ahead.

I stoop and crouch, pull and lift, move slowly along the paths, content in these weekly times of wandering in the silence. Birdsong is the only sound other than the rustle of deer or chipmunk or wild turkey—I even saw a horned owl once. I return to my room dirty, tired, and happy, to a warm shower and a good night's sleep.

At first, ashram gardeners explored new paths, marked them with plastic tape tied to trees, and then painted yellow blazes on the trunks. But now the paths are more defined, and the joy is to maintain them in these ever-changing woods. There are tricky places. In one clearing where the ferns take over each year, I must weed repeatedly, grasping bunches of ferns with both hands, pulling and tossing aside their green feathery softness. At a rest stop overlooking the pond, the new beaver dam floods the path several years in a row, so staff redirect the path and relocate the wooden bench to higher ground. In 2012, Hurricane Sandy toppled hundreds of trees. They lie in twisted, massive corkscrews that require months of clearing by sawyers and rerouting of trails.

Ultimately, regular use maintains these paths; it's hard for weeds to grow in compacted soil. Solitary walks by ashram folk gradually define these wandering trails. The steady tread of feet packs the earth, clears the way, reveals the pattern.

~

Years earlier, when I first began to follow this path from India, I asked the Teacher for a spiritual name, an Indian name that supports a higher purpose, as Sanskrit names often do. She gave me the name *Chandrabhaga*, which literally means "auspicious moon." The moon is beloved as an image of the Teacher, the one who reflects the sun of the Truth. The word describes the waning crescent moon, with its fragile tips in the air, the last vestige of the mind before it is absorbed in the great Self of Consciousness. Chandrabhaga is also the name of a sacred river, in the pilgrimage city of Pandharpur in the Indian state of Maharashtra. The crescent-shaped river encircles the temple to Lord Vitthal, the deity of the poet-saints of this ancient culture.

I use Chandrabhaga internally in meditation and in letters to my Teacher but don't use it publicly or at the ashram because so much of my work is with people internationally. A few years later, I'm inspired by the moon in meditation and write the Teacher a letter, asking to begin using my spiritual name. She responds that she likes Jennie, so I continue as before. Then one day in a large meeting, she asks me and another staff person to identify the date of a series of meetings. The other staff person gives the correct date, and as I remember, the Teacher takes a breath, looks at me, and says, "And Chandrabhaga says the date is . . ." I'm ecstatic at this unexpected gift; she has given me my name to use! Within 24 hours, I decide to change my name tag, the nameplate on my office door, and my email address. It becomes the name by which I am known as I begin to live into the auspicious light of this word, the subtle sheen of this now visible weft.

~

My last seven years at the ashram are especially productive and challenging as I'm assigned to create a new department for our international organization. I call on all my diversity and volunteer organizational experience to create a system of global volunteers to support the work of this department. My documentation and editorial skills serve me well as I write reports and create databases for the many matters to which our office responds daily. It is in this daily office work and relations with coworkers that I learn to practice the teachings and apply my insights. We learn to build a team working for the highest good for the benefit of all.

Each month the staff meets to create artistic mind maps of our milestones and accomplishments for the month. We break into groups by department, and the four of us sit around a table with a large sheet of newsprint, magic markers, glue, and imaginative props we have grabbed from the office. We decide on a theme, draw the design, then add our agreed-on activities. All the skill sets change: Who has the best handwriting? The attorney. Who knows how to draw a world map? The educator. Who has the best idea for a theme related to the holiday this month? The monk. Who can color within the lines? Often me. It's a fun, refreshing and creative way to celebrate the work, all in less than an hour. Some of our most passionate meetings involve deciding which poster from the past year is our favorite, which accomplishments most important to display in the boardwalk for all staff at the end-of-year celebration. I thrive in the wholeness of texture and color and ever-changing pattern of the fabric we are weaving together.

~

It is at the ashram in 2003 that I begin to study and practice Tai Chi in earnest. A Tai Chi master teaches the Tai Chi 24-form to students during one of the Teacher's visits to California. They bring it back to the ashram and hold classes several times a week. Tai Chi is a great way for staff to develop more strength, relaxation, and flexibility, to maintain a healthy body and mind, which then can be applied to our life and *seva*. I begin to attend the early morning classes regularly, gradually learn and refine the moves, and then study related forms, as taught by the more senior students. Soon we are practicing every morning on the patio outdoors down by the tall white pines.

Tai Chi Chuan is an ancient form of traditional Chinese medicine, along with acupuncture, massage, and herbal medicine. It is based on the Taoist principle of circular flow, *yin* and *yang*. Its main principles are *jing*, stillness, and *song*, ease. Tai Chi has been called meditation in motion, and I find Tai Chi practice a dependable thread to carry meditation into my daily life. I ground my body with steady balance, still my mind and heart, and focus on the present moment, to flow in whole fabric.

The flow of Tai Chi begins to heal my body by releasing stuck energy, places where I have been unconsciously holding tension, especially in my neck and shoulders. Waves of self-doubt surface, reflected in stiff, uncertain movements. Why won't my head move with my torso? It seems to have a mind of its own. I'm trying too hard. I feel like I can't do anything right! The more the instructors correct me, the more tightly I contract and the stiffer I become mentally and physically when the goal is to relax and "play" Tai Chi. I eventually choose to leave the class and resolve to practice on my own, to work through the negativity, to refine the moves by studying with videos. Slowly, after several months, my confidence returns, I relax and return to the group. Soon I begin to lead practice sessions, grateful for the renewed ease of mind and body.

As I practice in the cool mornings, surrounded by the scent of pine and the pale moon setting in the sky, I begin the form with a bow to the sun and align myself with a pine that reminds me to stand tall and straight and still before I flow into the moves, feet grounded in the earth and head suspended from the sky. The Chinese names of the moves inspire: I part the wild horse's mane, spread white stork wings, play the Chinese lute, repulse the monkey, grasp the sparrow's tail, flick the whip, wave hands like clouds, high pat the horse, creep down like a snake, balance on one leg like a golden rooster, kick and box ears, weave the shuttle as a jade maiden, pick up a needle at the bottom of the sea, part the Chinese fan, deflect, parry and punch, seal, cross arms, and return to emptiness.

Tai Chi

The body flows
    softly
        gently
            easefully

With the pulse of the breath,
    gathering inward,
        expanding outward,
            in the circle of life.

Yin and Yang,
    stillness and movement,
        beginning and ending with nothing—*wu*,
            in the middle, everything—*tai*.

The mind moves in focused stillness with the pulse,
    led by the body's memory of legs, torso, arms,
        chi flowing up from the earth to the *dantien*—
            red field below the navel,
        up the spine, out the hands, eyes, top of the head.

I am whole,
   beautiful,
      powerful,
         surrendered,
            aware.

Still like a mountain,
   flowing like a river,
      I play tai chi.

~

As I turn seventy in 2015 and the circle of life revolves, I begin to feel like it is time for me to move on. The ashram is a place for whole-hearted contribution, and I'm beginning to slow down. I plan a final visit to India, a silent retreat at the ashram in Maharashtra, preceded by a pilgrimage across the *desh*, the lush farmland of central India, to my namesake sacred river, Chandrabhaga. A friend who lives in the ashram in India and speaks Hindi and Marathi plans the trip for my travel companion and me. She serves as our guide, hires the van driver, reserves a room at the small Indian hotel in Pandharpur, and advises us on the food.

The driver is skilled at avoiding the potholes on the dusty dirt road leading to Pandharpur, the pathway for the pilgrims who twice a year walk the long spiritual journey to this sacred city to experience *darshan*, the presence of Lord Vitthal and his consort Rukmini. They walk in family and village groups, carry orange flags on tall poles, and carry a shrine. They sing songs I know from the ashram, the ecstatic songs of the ancient poet saints of the region: Jnaneshwar, Namdev, Janabai, Eknath, Tukaram, Mirabai.

We, too, are driving along this pilgrim's way through the sunny, verdant farmland, along fields of sugarcane, passing oxen with gaily painted horns who pull carts loaded with cut cane. Young boys sitting atop the precarious loads wave at us. Every few miles, we drive through a small multicolored village with vendors at the roadside. A small plot in the middle is reserved for pilgrims, who pitch their tents for the night.

Jet-lagged and filled with anticipation, we arrive in Pandharpur at sunset, just in time to walk down the stone steps to the river Chandrabhaga. To reach her crescent waters, we cross a long plateau of mud flats occupied by herds of donkeys. The river has been diminished to knee-high depth by a flood last year and littered with the offerings of multitudes of pilgrims. Disappointed and near tears, I return to the hotel for supper and sleep. I use the typical Indian bathroom, where I wash with the bucket of water and squat over the floor-level toilet—dusty, tired, and sad. This Chandrabhaga is dirty water, running low.

At 4 a.m. the next morning, I return to the river to bathe, copying the motions of the local women. I purchase from one of them a small candle on palm leaves and marigolds and offer it to float on the waters. Then I make an offering of water I've brought from the Temple in the ashram in the U.S. As I rotate slowly, chant mantras, and sprinkle the water, devotion returns, and I know the joy of worshipping in the waters whose name I bear.

When we walk up the hill, we find a long line winding around the temple, as pilgrims wait to enter, chanting familiar ancient hymns, "*Vitthala, Vitthala, Panduranga Vitthale!*" We are the only Western faces among the Indian pilgrims, noticeably taller than everyone around us. Within the interior walls of the ancient stone temple, we circle around and around for hours with the lines of pilgrims. When we reach the inner sanctum of the *murti*, statue of Lord Vitthal, I notice a beautiful goddess with a crescent moon overhead engraved in bronze relief at the entrance. I know she is Chandrabhaga and touch her with reverence. My mind is still as my body trembles with the bliss of a journey fulfilled. As we move on, we enter a large pavilion in the middle of the temple, where pilgrims are dancing in ecstasy, joining cross-hands and twirling around and around in joy. I, too, know that joy.

We leave that afternoon and arrive at the ashram in the evening, tired, content, and filled with wonder. My pilgrimage is complete. Now I can move into the silent retreat, then on into the final weft of my life, the fabric nearing completion.

10
Flowing Weave

In June 2015 at age seventy, I arrive in Asheville, North Carolina, to stay for a month with longtime friends Sandra and Anita, recently married now that the Supreme Court has made it legal. They take me in, give me a bed to sleep in, food to eat, directions to find my way until I'm ready to live on my own. I settle into an upstairs room with four rambunctious kittens they are fostering—another stray also lovingly fed and cared for. I require foster care: parents are dead, family scattered, no inheritance,

The meditation study group at my home in 2019.
Back, left to right: Sharada, Sandra, Kailash, Gayle, Cliff, and Liz.
Front: Padma, Julie, Jennie. Photo by Liz Albright.

basic Social Security income, and orphaned by years of separation from my Baltimore women's community. I'm starting over in a strange place. They offer tips on finding used furniture at estate sales, bed at a rummage sale, chair from a friend, old dresser polished to cover scratches, plates and utensils at the dollar store. Haltingly, I learn how to feed myself again, although I burn the beans the first time friends come for dinner. Thank God for cat lovers and forgiving, generous friends.

I arrive with a clear, yet broad-brush vision for my later years, in the form of a hand drawn mind map on my meditation shelf. It includes, as always, adopting a cat. Within a month the vision manifests. I move into a sunny, 750-square-foot rental house deep in a mountain valley along the South Toe River in Yancey County, about an hour north of Asheville. Here, the rents are much cheaper and the community is rich in artists, craftspeople, writers, and like-minded community.

I soon begin to volunteer at Dig In! Yancey Community Garden. I am recruited by a woman dressed as a big orange carrot at the annual Mt. Mitchell Craft Fair. I also sign up for the Carolina Mountains Literary Festival, join a local hiking group, a food coop, and drive up the road to Open Ridge farm to purchase organic fresh greens and other produce. I'm grateful to drive into Asheville regularly to visit my friends and to chant and meditate with the community of devotees there. They provide a vital connection with my ashram past, which supports my ashram service as an editor from home, along with daily meditation and chanting practice and visits to the path's website.

In August, I adopt Lily from the Yancey Humane Society, a warm feline companion who settles into my lap each evening as I sit in the wingback chair to journal, listen to music, and read. Cell phone and laptop are my only communication tools—no TV or land line. I'm happy in this simple life I've chosen. I want to slow down from my life of busy "doing" and cultivate space for more creativity, learn how to nurture myself, live simply, and build sustainable community for my later years.

Writing poetry and sharing it with others is new, and so is birdwatching. I'm returning to contra dancing after a 50-year absence. I grow my own small garden and learn to cook with local organic produce—all new. I've never cleaned out my own gutters before, perching high up on the ladder, broom in hand. I cook up natural dyes to color the Easter eggs this year—turmeric for gold, onion skins for red, red cabbage for blue—definitely new. I dust off old skills: organize an LGBTQ panel at the Friends Meeting to speak about scripture and use my archival and editing skills with the literary festival.

~

I find Dr. Larry Cammarata, a Tai Chi teacher in Asheville, become his assistant in weekly classes, and learn Qigong. Slowly, my Tai Chi practice expands and I'm certified as an instructor. I initiate teaching Tai Chi and Qigong classes on my own at the local Celo Health Center, grateful for sustained practice over the years and its fruits now. I'm learning to flow into this new pattern of living.

As I practice and teach Qigong and Tai Chi, I learn to integrate its basic principles into my practice, to trust my body's inner knowing of these truths, to connect with earth below, sky above, fire and water within, to flow in balanced, whole-body integration with the *spanda*, to weave my life into the pattern of creative pulsation that sustains the universe.

~

Connection with life of the spirit has many names—Holy Spirit in Christianity, *ruach/ruh* in Judaism and Islam, inner Light in Quakerism, *yin* ebb and *yang* flow of the *chi* in Taoism, pulsation of *spanda* and breath of *prana shakti* in my Indian yogic path. The truth of this ever-present inner and outer flow of life is beyond words and religions. As one expression of this flow, Yang Cheng-Fu (1883–1936), master teacher of Yang family Taijiquan, established the following ten key principles of Tai Chi, which I follow in my new life here in the mountains.

Vitality of Spirit Leads to the Top of the Head

I practice Tai Chi under the pine and pear trees in the front yard of my new home in the mountains of western North Carolina, soft pine needles under my feet. I stand facing a pine, align my spine with its upward thrust, slowly raise and lower my arms as I bend my knees, breathe deep into my belly. The *chi* flows up from the earth under my feet, up my legs to the *dantien* below my navel, and on up my spine, out my arms, eyes, and top of the head into the sky.

Arc Your Chest and Round Your Back

As I sit in front of the old four-harness Leclerc jack loom, I throw the shuttle, reach for the beater, and add another weft thread of shining turquoise, gold, or garnet wool to the patterned placemats I'm weaving, held by strong cotton warp threads in the same colors.

I'm still learning to weave on this loom. Neighbor Patti came over last week to help me thread the treadles and give wise advice on keeping the ends from tangling as I move the warp ends from warping board to loom. Now, I've finally completed the calculations, measuring, warping, beaming, threading, and tying. I delight in the even, taut rows of colorful stripes of warp ends ready to be woven, the even shed when I move the treadles with my feet.

I learn to create an even tension and weave, which calls for full body movement and coordination of arms, legs, and torso, along with sustained mental focus—seated Tai Chi, meditation in motion.

Loosen Your Waist and Hips

Just out the door and about a quarter mile down the mountain, the South Toe River winds its way through the valley beneath the Black Mountains. I follow the stream behind my house down its watershed into the river. The mixed pine and hardwood forest is dense with rhododendron, raspberry briars, galax, moss, and dog hobble. It's a scramble to walk directly down to the river, skirting the electric fence for the goats in the pasture next door and on down the pathless hill. I experiment with access routes. One way is to walk up the winding country two-lane highway, past the old trash dump with parked semi-trailers, to the next pullover, which opens into an overgrown, rutted dirt road down to the river.

In summer, I pick raspberries from the bushes along the trail down to the river and across the road up the power-line cut. I bend and twist to reach deep into the brambles for the juicy red and black berries, scratching up my arms and legs until I learn to wear long-sleeved shirts and pants on these walks.

Where the road ends at the river, I find the footpath along its banks, carefully step over small streams feeding into the water, tree roots, mud holes. I grab and hold onto roots as I slide down the steep bank to the river itself and sit on one of the large rocks at the edge of the water. I watch children in inner tubes from the campground on the other side, floating and splashing in the rushing, shallow stream. Rhododendrons lean out over the river and trees hug the bank, roots exposed to the clean, cold water. This is a perfect spot for wading or for sitting on the rock to munch an apple, enjoy the play of light on water, birdsong, minnows, the flow of life.

As I continue along the riverside path, I end at a clearing that takes me to a gravel road by neighbor Sarah's home and pottery studio. A few years back, her electrician husband installed the electricity at the renovation of my little house, formerly a bare-bones studio. We exchange cat-sitting when one of us is away; she barters with blueberries from the abundant bushes planted on their slope. I clamber down, stand on tiptoe, and squat on heels to pick the abundant bags of berries that I freeze to add to my morning oatmeal. I'm grateful for neighbors.

I walk up their drive, climb steeply past other homes, barns, and woodpiles to the highway, then past Powderhorn, Pinwheel, and finally to the mailboxes at Passional Way and down to my little green pointy-roof house with swing out front and neighbors down the hill. I've walked the loop, too much along the narrow highway, but delightful down to and along the river.

Distinguish Substantial and Insubstantial

I learn how to garden for myself and contribute to this mountain community by volunteering at Dig In! Yancey Community Garden, which grows and gives away fresh produce for the one in four people in Yancey County who don't always have enough to eat, supplementing the dried and canned goods at local food pantries. The other goal of Dig In! is to cooperate with local schools and organizations to teach young people how to grow their own food, a skill that is declining with the rise of fast-food burgers and takeout pizza.

On Thursday mornings, I drive to the large garden plot, generously offered by local folks, where raised beds, lasagna beds, containers, and row beds grow tomatoes, onions, carrots, sweet potatoes, lettuce, radishes, beets, sweet and hot peppers, corn, peas, okra, spinach, kale, collards, chard, and more.

Kathleen and Olivia, the two staff, receive helpful advice

and generous donations from local farmers and groups—from mulch to mowers to outhouses—and farm with the support of volunteers like me, who show up once a week for a morning or afternoon to dig, sow, weed, and harvest. On each visit I learn more—when to plant, how far apart, next to what, how and when to water, how to harvest, hang in the barn to season, mulch for next season, stake and tie up tomatoes and beans, measure and dig contoured rows for best drainage, label and store tools in the barn.

Sometimes I lead volunteers in Tai Chi warm-ups at the garden in the morning to loosen our arms and legs, open our lungs, and prepare for all the stooping and bending and pulling and hoeing—we call ourselves the mattock mavens.

Coached by Dig In! the first season, I prepare a lasagna bed in my back yard at the end of the drive on the sunny side next to the stream—laying down layers of cardboard, grass clippings, straw, and mulch. The next Spring, I plant tomato starts in black plastic containers ringed by basil, tomatillos, and beets from seed. The tomatoes take over, sprawling over the grass and driveway, giving me abundance to freeze, cook, barter, and give to friends. Slowly, I learn what to do and not do, to surrender to the voles, to unwind the garden hose for regular watering, and to accept haphazard sprouting. I learn to shift my weight from knee to knee as I reach deep into the leafy green for the red and golden fruit, discern ripe from unripe, split from whole, distinguish weed from food. This will feed me—this will not. This I throw in the mulch pile—this in the compost pile.

Sink the Shoulders and Drop the Elbows

I'm eager to explore the local trails, so I join the North Carolina High Peaks Trail Association for their monthly hikes along the Appalachian Trail, Mountains-to-Sea Trail, and Black Mountain trails. One of my first hikes is along the Crest Trail, from Mt. Mitchell, the highest peak in the East, to Deep Gap. I discover magnificent vistas of mountains and forest and rare wildflowers with easygoing and knowledgeable hiking companions. In addition to monthly hikes, the group maintains the AT, MST, and Black Mountain trails on Monday workdays each week and scavenges for litter at Blue Ridge Parkway overlooks. I choose Buck Creek Gap overlook as my litter spot. The gap, along the Eastern

Continental Divide, is where highway 80 South, along which I live, crosses the Blue Ridge Parkway and descends steeply down to Marion to the east, in a series of tortuous switchbacks known by local motorcyclists as "the devil's whip."

One of my favorite short solo hikes is along the Mountains-to-Sea Trail after it crosses the Parkway at Buck Creek Gap, up one of the U.S. Forest Service roads that interlace these mountains, and along the MST trail to a rocky outcropping with a 270-degree view of the mountains to the East. A friend saw a peregrine falcon build its nest there recently, and I once found a snakeskin on a rock where its owner had been sunning. Here I relax, breathe deep, eat my peanut butter and jam sandwich, lean back onto the rocks, and allow the sun and wind to relax my tight shoulders, soothe my mind. On my return to the gap parking lot, I stoop to pick up cigarette butts, soda cans, and other litter. The overlook is a favorite stop for the multitudes of motorcyclists and tourists traveling the Parkway—it's surprisingly clean most of the time, except for ubiquitous tobacco stubs.

Use your Yi-Mind Not Your Li-Strength

On Friday mornings I drive an hour to Asheville to assist my teacher Larry with Qigong and Tai Chi classes. There I practice the disciplines of mental focus, relaxation, and body awareness. I remember to remain grounded in the earth, my lower body heavy, feet planted firmly, knees slightly bent. I allow my upper body to be light, imagine the top of my head suspended from the sky by a golden cord. In this way I release any upper-body tension so my center of gravity, and thus balance, is lower and my breath deeper, supporting strength and flexibility. I've practiced this discipline for years, gradually becoming attuned to each part of my body, its weight, movement, relation to the whole. The more slowly I move, the more mental focus I gather, body and mind merged in easeful flow with the present. I notice where I hold tension—often my left shoulder—where the path is blocked, when and where I waver in balance, where and when my mind wanders, and continue to integrate all of me into this meditation in motion.

Upper and Lower Body Follow Each Other

Crest Trail

I hike along the summits of these towering, ancient mountains—
    historic Mitchell, Craig, Big Tom,
    Balsam Cone, Cattail Peak, Potato Hill,
Then steeply down to Deep Gap;
    leave Winter Star, Gibbs and Celo Knob for another day.

Up I puff,
    down I clamber
On miles of rocky, leaf-covered trail,
    in the crisp, blue morning air,
Ancient mountains of fiery color
    spread below me.

Along the crest of this glory
    I watch each step,
        alert to the ground before me.
Rock and Sky
        Earth and Heaven
            joined in each breath.

Harmonize Your Mind and Body

After 15 years of eating three delicious vegetarian meals a day prepared by ashram cooks, one of my goals is to learn how to cook for myself, grow my own garden, and buy local organic produce. These mountains offer abundant support—pear and apple trees in the yard, blackberries and blueberries across the road and up the hill, a small garden for greens, beets, lettuce, tomatoes, and basil at the end of the driveway.

    I soon find Open Ridge farm, up the road a bit, where Jona, Gretchen, and daughter Opal grow organic greens and vegetables, which I purchase from the email checklist they send, picked fresh that morning. They make their living selling produce to local restaurants, at the Burnsville Farmer's Market on Saturday mornings, and to neighbors like me who pick up our orders at the farm. I experiment with the different greens and vegetables they grow—kohlrabi, wax beans, fingerling potatoes, many varieties of summer and winter squash. And so, I learn to cook from what is fresh, augmented by the local food coop's bulk room for staples like cornmeal, split yellow mung beans, steel-cut oats, and cartons of local eggs.

Supplied with staples, fresh produce, and cookbooks from friends—*Tassajara Cooking* and *Cooking the Whole Foods Way* my favorites—I set aside Tuesdays as cooking day and learn how to cook a week's supply of some of my ashram favorites. I cook oatmeal with fresh fruit and nuts for breakfast. For supper, I eat *kichadi*—mung beans and rice with the Indian "magic" spices of mustard, cumin, fennel, coriander, and turmeric, eaten with pickled veggies and wilted greens. To create my favorite ashram salad dressing, I dice fresh garlic to add to tahini and lemon.

I have fun baking quick breads, weekly experiments in fresh, hot bread for every meal and for potlucks. I bake cornbread in the cast-iron skillet—without sugar here in the southern mountains according to local author Ronni Lundy's *Victuals*. The next week, it's cottage cheese/walnut muffins from the 1982 vegetarian cookbook sister Susan gifted me. Then cranberry/granola scones, buttermilk biscuits with dill, and more.

I learn to put by—to pickle vegetables, preserve ginger bean chowchow, ginger pear chutney, pear butter, freeze beans and zucchini in large plastic bags. I pick raspberries and abundant blackberries up the hill along the power cut and freeze them for plopping into my oatmeal on winter mornings. The top shelf of the fridge is filled with jars of preserved fruit and veggies. The freezer is filled with bags of frozen green vegetables, cherry tomatoes, and blueberries.

That first autumn, I discover two old pear trees in the front yard, harvest the windfall, and discover the many delights of pear, to give away, preserve, slice into oatmeal, bake with granola, and more. I invite friends over to harvest pear and haul bushels to Dig In! to distribute at local harvest tables.

Lunch is the main and most experimental meal. I try soups, casseroles, and stews served over brown rice, quinoa, pasta, couscous, barley, and other grains. I soak and cook with lima beans, kidney beans, black beans, and garbanzos. It's such a delight to experiment, hunt through recipe books, adapt to what I have on hand, feed my body and stimulate my mind with new foods, seasonings, and tastes—a daily adventure in self-nurture.

Continuity Without Break

We conclude our weekly Tai Chi class at the Celo Health Center by practicing the Tai Chi 24-form outside in the lower parking lot down near the South Toe River. In the still air of early evening, our music is rush of river, call of Carolina Wren, and silence of Black Mountains on the horizon.

We line up facing a tall oak, another tree to the back and one on each side—our rooted sentinels. My assistant Sandy leads at the front left and I take the right back corner, the newer folks in the middle to follow easily as we turn. After focus on details and practice of new moves during class, now we relax, breathe deep, and empty our minds.

We begin with the words, "still like a mountain, flowing like a river."

Our hands and feet, elbows and knees, shoulders and hips move in harmony with the form and with each other, our internal *chi* guiding us to flow together like a flock of birds, a school of fish.

Look for the Tranquil in Motion

I wake with the dawn, Lily the cat's warmth curled at my knees, look out the window, seeking golden, crimson sunrise, listen to the chip . . . chip . . . chip . . . of cardinals in the morning air, breathe in and out gently, repeat a mantra to welcome the day.

Once persistent Lily is fed, I splash water on my face, pull on jeans and T-shirt, unplug the iPhone, make the bed. Now I stand before the meditation space in the corner of the bedroom, wave a light to the Teacher and the dancing Shiva Nataraj, inhale and exhale slowly as I loosen my body with gentle Qigong stretches. I sit cross-legged on a white wool cushion, wrap a warm turquoise shawl around my shoulders, read words of wisdom from my Teacher, and close my eyes to meditate. I breathe in and out three times, holding each finger and my palms, 36 breaths to still mind and body and relax into silence. In this silence, the fire of the *shakti* radiates up my back and head, creates and dissolves thoughts, clears the path for my day. As I fold up my shawl, Lily purrs up to me, nudges for a gentle stroke under her chin. I choose a virtue from the stack of cards—today is *sthairya*, constancy.

My morning Tai Chi practice sustains me in this vibrant

stillness. I follow the path into my day—cook oatmeal, drive on winding roads, harvest garden turnips, chat at potluck, ponder a sentence structure, complete an online survey, marvel at the upside-down peck of the nuthatch, journal in the easy chair at day's end. I breathe as I weave.

"Still like a mountain, flowing like a river," I play Tai Chi in 2016.
Photo by Dr. Larry Cammarata.

11
Remnants

Coverlet

During the warmer months, a pieced quilt top covers the day bed in the living room of my new mountain home. Mother passed it on to me after Grandma Isla Mae Boyd died of Alzheimer's. Isla Mae stitched it from Grampy Jim's shirts, rectangles of white, gray, blue, and beige cotton in subtle checks and stripes, machine sewn with no edging—a scrap really, but large enough to cover the mattress. I mend tears from the cat's claws, wash and put it away each winter, and have saved it for over 40 years.

Isla Mae Splawn and James Cleveland Boyd were married on stage at their graduation from Decatur Baptist College in East Texas. She was the daughter of a Baptist preacher and soon to become preacher's wife. They raised one son and five daughters: JC Jr., Jennie (my mom), Elizabeth, Ruth, 'Cile, and Ann. The family story is that Grampy Jim managed a Baptist hospital in Fort Worth that went bankrupt during the Depression, forcing the family to move to a small church in Spurger, Texas, a come-down that "like ta killed" Grandmother. They settled on a farm near the small town of Center in East Texas when he retired. Grampy Jim, known as "Brother Boyd" at prayer meetings in town, raised livestock and chickens. Grandmother hosted teas for church ladies, tended the goats and produce garden, and taught manners to growing numbers of visiting grandchildren.

I'm surrounded by the Boyd women's legacy of hard work, hand-crafted covers, and make-do generosity. Before she died, Aunt 'Cile gave me her first cross-stitch project, a small square pillow with yellow and gold pansies. It sits in the rocking chair across from the Boyd coverlet. She also sold me her 1991 Honda

Civic, which I drove for 15 years. Mother gave me her name—Jennie Boyd. I eat on what is left of Mother's china, stacked in the dish drainer. In warm weather, I meditate beneath her prized blue Thai silk shawl, now hanging on the wall in the corner of my bedroom.

Bench

The dark brown walnut bench with curved edges rests in front of the couch. It is low enough to hold mugs of tea and to prop up my feet when I read evenings in the wingback chair. Several stains on the top from misplaced mugs and a hairline crack at one end reveal its years of use. I rub it with Murphy's oil several times a year to keep the wood clean, working for a dull sheen.

On days off from pastoring at St. James in Knoxville, Father crafted the bench decades ago in his workspace down in the basement. He gave me the bench on a trip home to Knoxville in the 1970s. I've used it in the living room all my adult life, hauling it from place to place to sit in front of chairs and sofas and fireplaces, along with the matching lamp base he crafted of the same walnut.

His mother Gertrude Cornish Bull, another preacher's wife, this one Episcopalian from low country South Carolina, stitched the warm, golden needlepoint pillow with dogwood blossoms that sits in the wingback chair. The yellow sunflower she painted for me when I was a child rests on top of the bookcase next to the spider plant and Internet extender. Her large, framed watercolor of a white magnolia bud hangs between the bathroom and bedroom, a more recent gift from brother John after Father died. On Monday mornings, as I sit with my feet propped on the bench, John and I check in for our weekly phone call. These days he rides the bus and is a respected advocate for public transportation in Nashville and for unhoused folks in his neighborhood. I brag about John's daily Tai Chi practice and new veggie garden on his patio.

Rug

A handwoven brown-and-white rug catches splatters between sink and stove in my kitchen during the summer. In winter months, I move it under the table where I eat, looking out the picture window at the cardinals and nuthatch on the feeder.

Woven in the traditional overshot pattern of the Southern mountains, eyes of alternating ovals stare up from the floor, a few eyes now in tatters. I love the names of these mountain patterns: Honeysuckle, Star and Rose, Enigma, Trellis, Patchwork, and Monk's Belt.

Weaving is a traditional craft of the Southern mountains. Penland School of Crafts, in nearby Mitchell County, began in the 1920s when Lucy Morgan traveled to Berea College in Kentucky to learn to weave. On her return, she founded the Penland Weavers, a cottage industry that gave local women looms and yarn and then marketed their handweaving.

The brown-and-white rug was a gift when I was Minister of Outreach with Metropolitan Community Church in Washington, DC, in the early 1980s. When I moved into one of the many garret-roofed attic apartments I've lived in over the years, a woman in the church gave me a hundred-dollar check to buy something I wanted for my new home. I splurged on the rug at a craft store in upscale Georgetown that sold handweaving from the mountains. The overshot rug has been part of my life ever since and a reminder of my Southern mountain roots.

I worked in Hazard, Kentucky, with AFSC after college, where I bought the rocking chair in the living room from a stand along a country road. The green-and-white trellis-patterned runner is another Kentucky gift from Berea. It always covers the top of my dresser, these days shredded in the back right corner, where I left a potted plant for too long one year. The smaller green rug in the same overshot pattern was my first weaving purchase at Hindman School in 1970. It's now a worn and comfy mat for Lily the cat in her hideaway, a big cardboard Chewy cat food box.

Placemats

Deep red, fringed, hand-loomed placemats and napkins lie on the table where I eat daily, the overshot rug underneath. The mats, woven in Berea, were a Christmas gift from Linda when I pastored the MCC congregation in Baltimore in the 1980s. They alternate with the newer pink placemats made in China, which I picked up at Barkin' Basement in Burnsville. The wooden ladderback chair with woven rush seat at the table was a gift from Linda's mom one Christmas, a match for the rocking chair.

North Carolina was the textile capital of the U.S. for many years until fabric manufacturing shipped overseas to Asia and mills shut down all over the state. Here in Yancey County there are remnants. Glen Raven is one of the largest industries in the county, weaving technical fabric like flags, umbrellas, pantyhose. Textile plants were the precursors of computers; Jacquard looms used punch cards to pattern the weave, prototype for the punch cards used in the first mainframe computers. Yet, the mountains of Appalachia continue to draw weavers and fabric artists. Walk into any craft store and you'll find multicolored handwoven scarves and shawls, mats and rugs displayed amongst the pottery. At the recent Celo Community Center yard sale, an old four-harness floor loom sat in the driveway, $300 price tag attached.

Linda was a generous and creative companion for many years. Her hand-thrown pots, scattered around the house, hold shells, daisies, rubber bands, ripening tomatoes. She gifted me with three of my favorite handwoven tops. They hang in the closet, in purple, blue/pink, and aqua/maroon twill and tabby weaves. I wear them often, along with the long turquoise velour bathrobe she sent for Christmas the year I left for the ashram. I wrap it around me on chilly evenings. At night, Lily and I snuggle under the deep red comforter from our Baltimore home.

I weave my own placemats now, on the loom at the end of the kitchen counter. In the upper cabinet by the rocking chair, large, colorful spools of textured wool rug yarn stack the shelves, remnants from a rug factory in Hendersonville that moved downstate. Four placemats and napkins in checkered rust, turquoise, and gold stretch taut on the loom, woven intermittently over the past year, now patiently waiting for me to untie, cut, and hem them into use.

Shawls

The far corner of my bedroom holds a quiet space for meditation each morning. The Teacher's dark brown eyes shine with love from her photo on the low bookcase, covered with a vivid orange and gold silk shawl she gave me when I lived at the ashram. Another of her shawls, in a subtle floral pattern of ocher silk, the color of the swami robes she wears, hangs behind my meditation seat in winter months. Her soft, dark red pillow supports my back as I meditate.

Those fifteen years serving at the Teacher's ashram surrounded me with her presence, teachings, and the daily schedule of chanting, meditation, and service. I held monthly calls with devotees from every continent to sustain a spiritual community supported by daily postings on the path's website, global live webcasts, and ashrams, centers, and chanting/meditation groups around the world. Now that I've retired here to the mountains, three times a month I drive an hour to the group of devotees in Asheville to chant, meditate, and study her teachings. This year the theme is *Satsang*, the company of the Truth.

The majority of devotees live in India, where the shawls in my home were woven. I have visited the Teacher's ashram in Maharashtra three times over the past thirty years, a pilgrimage to my heart in days of silent retreat. On my last trip in 2014 I purchased a deep turquoise wool shawl to wrap around my shoulders as I meditate. The faint musky scent of Indian wool encases me each morning in remembrance.

Ashram life introduced me to Tai Chi, a daily practice for the past fifteen years. A Tai Chi long sword stands propped in the corner behind the rocker, its navy blue carrying case sporting the Wu Tao Kuan patch of my first teacher. I practice the Chen sword form in the open strip of floor between the couch and table, facing the day bed. The trekking pole and rubber yoga mat leaning alongside the sword were also ashram acquisitions, for Monday hikes in the mountains and morning yoga sessions. Sword, pole, and mat continue to support me here as I teach weekly Tai Chi classes, hike along mountain trails, and stretch in yoga.

Useful gifts from friends fill my home with memories of their kindness: Sonam's toaster oven and Barney's ceramic bowl on the kitchen counter, Ganga's wooden file trays in the bookcase, Gayle's boom box in the cabinet, Neha's wooden lyre by the window, Sandra and Anita's couch behind the bench and Bindu's blue mosaic tile from Turkey on the bench.

When I first arrived here, sister Susan and brother Thanh visited to welcome me. Susan lives in California with her son and his family and is a proud new great-grandmother, with three children and nine grandchildren. An excellent cook, she brought me a vegetarian cookbook, a salad spinner, a cast iron skillet, and her recipe for broccoli soup. She also passed on to me four much-needed pairs of jeans, since my wardrobe was lacking in these mountain-wear essentials. We share recipes and check in regularly by text. I love her sense of humor. Thanh and his wife Loan now live in Nashville, near two of their three children, two of whom are physicians. They are kind Buddhists, proud of their successful children and growing family. I'm grateful to reconnect with my brothers and sister in retirement.

~

Not only have placemats gone global, manufactured in China for North Carolina tables, but spiritual paths also interweave around the world. A preacher's kid from Knoxville now follows an Indian spiritual path, travels to India for retreats, and attends Celo Friends Meeting. A woman raised in India, now an international Guru, lives in an ashram in the eastern United States and offers global webcasts in multiple languages. I learn Tai Chi from a Chinese master at an Indian ashram and now teach in health clinics in Western North Carolina. The weave of liberation has shifted from my feminist, coming-out years in the 1970s,

Remnants, 2021.

when I discarded stereotypes to throw kicks in Tae Kwon Do, transformed into the gentle flow of Tai Chi today, relaxing into meditation in motion.

A brick-red wool shawl from my first pilgrimage to India over twenty-five years ago covers the back of the couch, its embroidered blue-and-orange leaves faded in spots. It rests beneath the cat painting, in front of the bench, next to the coverlet, across from the placemats and rug and sword. Lily wraps her paws in its rough texture when she plays in the twilight.

Epilogue
Tying Off

I've woven about two and a half feet of fabric on the loom, six inches in width. This sample piece of turquoise warp interweaves tabby weft of burnt orange, deep blue, aqua, and purple yarns. As I experiment with textures and colors and thicknesses, I soon learn that one of the essential skills is sustaining an even tension. The selvedges on the edges must be aligned and tight, not drawing in or hanging out in ragged nubs, as on this sample. Still, I'm proud of this, my first piece. I untie the warp threads from the back beam, pull them through the heddles and reed, and then tie them in groups of five ends, to create a thick turquoise fringe. Once tied off in the back, I then untie the threads from the front beam and create a fringe on the other end, cutting the fringe evenly with my sewing shears.

I hang the sample piece at the end of my bookcase, suspended at the top by a porcelain vase—a parting gift from the meditation center in Baltimore many years ago. It flows past two shelves of meditation books and ends halfway down at the shelf holding recent books of interest—poetry, memoir, Tai Chi, guides to birds, wildflowers, and trees of the Southern Appalachians.

When I pluck the turquoise yarn fuzz from the reed, the loom startles, naked with its lack of color. These days, I experience satisfaction at the weaving, awareness of skills to be refined, and that same vulnerable emptiness as I learn to surrender to this worn and rusting frame of a body. With what colors shall I weave the fabric of my life here in the mountains? I find myself opening a basket of yarns holding the colors and textures of past interests and skills, with new colors waiting to be discovered and interwoven. Trusted turquoise and gold colors and textures mingle with the greens and blues of the new weft as I weave this end fabric, replace threads that fray and break and tie off others, warp thread by groups of warp threads.

> Old loom stands at counter's end,
> > Worn wood frame, rusty steel reed,
> > Slender heddles dangling.
> > Naked with age,
> > Waiting for warp of color,
> > Weft of yarn
> > > to weave into life.

Woven placemats on the loom, 2019.

Works Cited

Chapter 3

Women: A Journal of Liberation, Winter 1970, vol 1 #2, What Is Liberation? "High School Women: Oppression and Liberation," Jennie Boyd Bull.

Ibid., Winter 1971, vol 2 #2, "How We Live as Toads," Jennie Boyd Bull, Marilyn Clark, Anne Coulter.

Chapter 4

Diana Press flyer, Baltimore, January 1972.

Women Against Daddy Warbucks flyer, New York, July 3, 1969.

Palm of Your Hand: a collection of writings and drawings by lesbians from Baltimore and elsewhere. (Diana Press, 1972).

Songs to a Handsome Woman, Rita Mae Brown. (Diana Press, Baltimore, MD, 1973).

Feminist Views of Christianity: A Study Guide and Reader, Jennie Boyd Bull, ed. (Mother Eagle Press, UFMCC, 1977).

"Our God Is Like an Eagle," lyrics by Larry Bernier, UFMCC.

Chapter 5

Making a Way: Lesbians Out Front, Photographs by JEB (Joan E. Biren), p. 21 (Glad Hag Books, Washington, DC, 1987).

Chapter 6

"Gay Church Again Rejected by National Council Group," Dennis Hevesi (*New York Times*, Nov. 15, 1992).

Chapter 7

Publishers Weekly, Sept. 6, 1991. "Success Story: Baltimore's 31st Street Bookstore," pp. 68–70.

The Disappearing L: Erasure of Lesbian Spaces and Culture, Bonnie J. Morris (SUNY Press, 2016).

Chapter 9

Sri Guru Gita, verse 110, author's unpublished translation, 2010.

"Tai Chi," *Where I Live: Coming Home to the Southern Mountains*, Jennie Boyd Bull (Finishing Line Press, Georgetown, KY, 2018).

Chapter 10

Victuals: An Appalachian Journey, with Recipes, Ronni Lundy (Penguin/Random House, New York City, 2016).

"Crest Trail," *Where I Live: Coming Home to the Southern Mountains*, Jennie Boyd Bull (Finishing Line Press, Georgetown, KY, 2018).

About the Author

Jennie Boyd Bull retired to the mountains of Western North Carolina in 2015 at age seventy, following careers as an editor at the National Trust for Historic Preservation, pastor with Metropolitan Community Church of Baltimore, manager of the feminist 31st Street Bookstore, librarian with Baltimore County Public Libraries, and editor, archivist, and department head in an ashram in the U.S. She received a B.A. in English Literature from Swarthmore College in 1967 and an M.Div. from Wesley Theological Seminary in 1982. In 1992, she received the Passages Community Service Award for 20 years of service in the Baltimore and Washington lesbian communities.

Raised in Knoxville, Tennessee, Jennie is grateful to have returned home to the Appalachians, where she volunteers with the Carolina Mountains Literary Festival, the NAACP, Dig In! Yancey Community Garden, MY Neighbors eldercare network, and Celo Friends Meeting. A Tai Chi instructor, she teaches Qigong and Tai Chi in the Toe River Valley. Her poetry chapbook, *Where I Live: Coming Home to the Southern Mountains*, was published by Finishing Line Press in 2018, and her poetry has appeared in several North Carolina periodicals. When she is not meditating or writing or weaving, she's hiking mountain trails, weeding out back in the garden, or curled up reading with Lily the cat.

www.ingramcontent.com/pod-product-compliance
Lightning Source LLC
Chambersburg PA
CBHW022019290426
44109CB00015B/1234